ERIC/OSEP Mini-Library

Adapting Curricular Materials

D0630235

Adapting Language Arts, Social Studies, and Science Materials for the Inclusive Classroom

B. Keith Lenz and
Jean B. Schumaker

CEC

Published by
The Council for Exceptional Children

ERIC

A Product of the
ERIC/OSEP Special Project
The ERIC Clearinghouse on
Disabilities and Gifted Education

Library of Congress Cataloging-in-Publication Data

Adapting language arts, social studies, and science materials for the
    inclusive classroom : grades six through eight / Jean Schumaker and
    Keith Lenz [editors].
        p.   cm. — (Adapting curricular materials ; v. 3)
    Includes bibliographical references.
    ISBN 0-86586-340-7
        1. Handicapped children—Education (Middle school)—United States.
    2. Language arts (Middle school)—United States.   3. Social
    sciences—Study and teaching (Middle school)—United States.
    4. Science—Study and teaching (Middle school)—United States.
    5. Inclusive education—United States.   I. Schumaker, Jean B.
    II. Lenz, B. Keith.   III. Series.
    LC4028.A33   1999
    371.9′044—dc21   99-12954
                                                                            CIP

ISBN 0-86586340-7

A product of the ERIC/OSEP Special Project, the ERIC Clearinghouse on
Disabilities and Gifted Education.

Published in 1999 by The Council for Exceptional Children, 1920 Association
Drive, Reston, Virginia 20191-1589

Stock No. P5307

This publication was prepared with funding from the U.S. Department of
Education, Office of Special Education Programs, contract no. ED-99-CO-0026.
Contractors undertaking such projects under government sponsorship are
encouraged to express freely their judgment in professional and technical
matters. Prior to publication the manuscript was submitted for critical review
and determination of professional competence. This publication has met such
standards. Points of view, however, do not necessarily represent the official
view or opinions of either The Council for Exceptional Children or the Department of Education.

Printed in the United States of America
10 9 8 7 6 5 4 3 2

Contents

PART II: EXAMPLES OF MATERIAL ADAPTATIONS

Preface

Teachers in inclusive classrooms regularly face the difficult task of having to modify the curriculum to reach all of their students, many of whom have special needs. Students with disabilities, whether physical, emotional, or cognitive in nature, respond to the curriculum differently from other students. For example, depending on the disability itself and other factors affecting their ability to succeed academically, students may need modifications such as advance and graphic organizers, instructional scaffolding, additional practice and time to complete assignments, and/or alternative media (e.g., large-print materials, audiotapes, or electronic materials). Without specific modifications, the standard curricular materials can be inadequate for these students, and too frequently they can find themselves blocked from access to essential aspects of the curriculum. Teachers must adjust the materials or their presentation to break down the barriers and assist these students in learning.

The IDEA Amendments of 1997 require that students with disabilities have access to the general education curriculum. This legislative requirement makes the accessibility of curricular materials an issue of even greater importance than it otherwise would be. To meet the goal of equal access to the curriculum for everyone, to enable each student to engage with his or her lessons in a meaningful way, teachers must be prepared to provide useful alternatives in terms of both curricular materials and instructional delivery. Well-adapted materials without an effective method of teaching are practically useless, but with the proper tools and instructional methods, a good teacher encourages each member of the class to participate directly in the learning experience.

Unfortunately, teachers who have to work with standard, off-the-shelf curricular materials usually have little time to develop accommodations for their classes. They need a guidebook that outlines successful adaptation strategies in clear, concise language, something that demonstrates the link between purpose and procedure for a teacher in a classroom of diverse learners. This ERIC/OSEP Mini-Library was designed to fill the gap for educators who are already engaged in curriculum adaptations as well as those who have not yet begun. The three volumes in this series:

- Outline the conceptual strategies behind instructional adaptations.

- Present characteristics of classroom materials that allow for effective adaptations.

- Illustrate those adaptations in brief, process-oriented chapters and vignettes. The adaptations describe best or promising practices that are based upon relevant special education research.

The Mini-Library consists of three books:

1. An introductory overview on general principles of adaptation of curricular materials, written by Edward J. Kame'enui and Deborah Simmons of the University of Oregon.

2. A volume on adaptation for kindergarten through fifth-grade, using the content-areas of reading and math, by Jeanne Shay Schumm of the University of Miami.

3. A volume on adaptation in grades three through eight, in language arts, social studies, and science, by Jean Schumaker and Keith Lenz of the University of Kansas.

Clearly, three short volumes cannot cover the range of disabilities and other diverse learning needs that teachers have to confront. We have limited our consideration to mild cognitive disabilities and have focused on adapting materials rather than on delivery (although in practice the two go hand in hand). For those who wish to read more about adaptations, the books provide references to additional resources on effective teaching methods and research.

A Word on Universal Design

This Mini-Library proceeds from the assumption that teachers who have to adapt instruction for their students usually don't have a say in choosing the curriculum or designing the materials before they are expected to use them. This series of publications offers the means to facilitate that process. If the developers of curricular materials anticipated some of the needs that teachers face in inclusive classrooms, such as students who read below grade level or who have organizational or attention-deficit problems, and if they then designed accommodations for these needs into the materials, that would free up teachers to devote more time to teaching and less to adapting the curriculum. While this may sound like an ideal situation, actually it is neither unrealistic nor far in the future of public school classrooms. Over the past few years, there has been a concerted effort in special education to promote curricular materials with built-in adaptations, particularly in digital media, that are flexible and customizable. Known as *universal design for learning*, the movement is based on the principles behind the universal design movement for access to products and environments for all users, regardless of sensory or physical disabilities.

The educational strategies behind universal design for learning basically underlie any sort of classroom adaptations. When a teacher adapts a curriculum, she or he works to accommodate as many student needs as possible by developing an array of potential supports. An unadapted curriculum generally is one-size-fits-all, but adapted materials can be tailored to the students. In this way, universally designed materials can accommodate students where they need it, but those supports are incorporated during the development phase, rather than having to be added after the fact. The same strategies that teachers use to adapt inefficient or inconsiderate materials go into universally designed curricular materials. A history text, for example, is written to include graphic organizers and strategic questions to help students who would find a typical text inaccessible but also to provide a challenge for those who would otherwise find it boring or unengaging. A digital reading program can highlight the text word for word or sentence by sentence for students who have difficulty following along by themselves, or it can say the words out loud for those who need more familiarity with the sounds of what they read. Such adaptations could be designed and provided by teachers—and this Mini-Library provides a number of successful examples—but the more resources that come packaged with the curriculum, the greater its flexibility and the less it has to be modified by the teacher.

Although materials that incorporate aspects of universal design have yet to become routine in schools, school districts in several states already are using preadapted books and digital media in their classrooms. For example, under a Department of Education grant, the Center for Applied Special Technology (CAST) is currently working with the State of New Hampshire to study the potential of technology to promote literacy for all students. This project, now implemented in 16 New England schools, uses a CD-ROM-based instructional program, *WiggleWorks*, that employs principles of universal design for learning. Other states, such as Texas and California, are using such preadapted, technology-supported programs for curriculum delivery. As technology inevitably plays an increasingly central instructional role, the concept of universal design for learning will gain prominence.

A Final Word on Adaptations

No computer or other classroom tool, no adapted materials can ever take the place of the teacher. Without an informed and dedicated teacher directing the learning, without someone who knows the students well enough to know what barriers to break down and where and how much to challenge a student, then even the best tools will be useless. Universally designed and adapted curricular materials are intended to provide teachers with more time and better means to get the job done, not to do the job for them.

Acknowledgments

Many people contribute their invaluable time and skills to a project such as this, and they need to be acknowledged. This Mini-Library resulted from a need to update a popular publication on curricular adaptations developed 10 years ago by the ERIC/OSEP Special Project. In late 1997, the Special Project, under the aegis of and with the support of the Office of Special Education Projects (OSEP), convened a group of researchers and practitioners to discuss the best ways to address the need for adapted materials in the inclusive classroom. Those intensive discussions and subsequent suggestions resulted in the outline for this series of books. We extend our appreciation to the researchers and teachers involved in the initial stages of this project and to authors Kame'enui, Lenz, Schumaker, Schumm, and Simmons, who agreed to devote a large portion of their time to this project in addition to their regular duties. We hope this Mini-Library will be a valuable tool for both special and general educators.

The manuscripts were graciously and carefully reviewed by a number of practitioners and researchers in the field. Their comments helped us to help the authors tighten the expression of their ideas. Special thanks are extended to Louise Appel, Pamela Burrish, Russell Gersten, Kathy Haagenson, Pauletta King, John Lloyd, Patricia Mathes, and Elba Reyes.

Special appreciation goes to Lou Danielson, director of OSEP's Research to Practice Division, whose commitment to these activities is borne out by his participation at each stage of development. The staff of the ERIC/OSEP Special Project at The Council for Exceptional Children were responsible for the meeting described previously and for conceptualizing and editing the three volumes. They are Kathleen McLane, Ray Orkwis, and Jane Burnette. All of us involved in developing these materials hope you will find them useful in your work, and we welcome your responses.

Nancy Safer
Executive Director
The Council for Exceptional Children

Introduction

Many students, especially those with disabilities, reach the middle grades with large skill deficits. On the average, they read at the fourth-grade level, cannot write complete sentences consistently, do not have fluent knowledge of the basic math facts, and have difficulty remembering information (Deshler & Schumaker, 1983). They do not know how to organize information (Bulgren, Hock, Schumaker, Deshler, & 1995) or how to organize their time (Hughes, Deshler, Ruhl, & Schumaker, 1993). Such skill deficits are a great disadvantage for students with disabilities who are included in the general education classroom at the middle-school level. In this setting they are typically expected to read textbooks written at the sixth-grade level and higher, write paragraphs and reports, keep track of and complete homework assignments, and study for and take tests in several subject areas.

While instructional methods are available for teaching many of these students the skills and strategies they need to be successful in the general education classroom in middle school, in high school, and beyond (Schumaker & Deshler, 1992), they take time and must be extensive as well as intensive (Deshler & Schumaker, 1993). How can you, as a teacher, support these students during this time so that they do not fail in their general education classes?

One effective method of support is to provide accommodations for these students. *Accommodations* are procedures or enhancements that enable a person with a disability to complete a task that he or she would otherwise be unable to complete because of a disability. One important accommodation for students in middle-school classrooms is material adaptations.

What Are Material Adaptations?

Material adaptations are alterations made in the materials that students use to learn or that teachers use to teach. These alterations become necessary when the materials currently being used present a barrier to student success. Adaptations can entail altering either the content or the format of the materials.

- *Content adaptations* involve changing the nature or amount of what will be learned. For example, instead of acquiring social studies concepts through a study of the relationships between countries, the learner acquires similar concepts through a study of the relationships between class members.

- *Format adaptations* involve changing the way information is presented to the learner. For example, instead of acquiring social studies concepts through independently reading a text about the relationships between European countries, the learner acquires the same concepts and the same content through listening to structured audiotapes and following a structured listening guide.

For students with mild cognitive disabilities, adaptations should be used primarily as a short-term solution to increase access to the curriculum and increase the probability that the student will be able to complete an academic task. They should not become a permanent substitute for the intensive instruction in important skills and strategies that students with disabilities need in order to become independent learners and performers. Short-term adaptations usually are introduced into classroom situations to enable learning, either by removing barriers to students' cognition or until they can be taught a skill or strategy that will enable them to learn independently. Some short-term adaptations may become permanent adaptations if needed by a particular student.

Effective adaptations also take time for teachers to design and implement. Ideally, the needed adaptations would be designed into the curricular materials by the developers, and the range of use of these preadapted materials would be broad enough to assist students regardless of their disability. When materials that employ such universal design elements are used in inclusive classrooms, they can minimize the amount and depth of adaptations that teachers need to make. The access is built into the design, rather than teachers being required to add it on afterwards.

References

Bulgren, J. A., Hock, M. F., Schumaker, J. B., & Deshler, D. D. (1995). The effects of instruction in a paired associates strategy on the information mastery performance of students with learning disabilities. *Learning Disabilities Research and Practice, 10*(1), 22–37.

Deshler, D. D., & Schumaker, J. B. (1983). Social skills of learning disabled adolescents: Characteristics and intervention. *Topics in Learning and Learning Disabilities, 3*(2), 15–23.

Deshler , D. D., & Schumaker, J. B. (1993). Strategy mastery by at-risk students: Not a simple matter. *The Elementary School Journal, 94,* 153–167.

Hughes, C. A., Deshler, D. D., Ruhl, K. L., & Schumaker, J. B. (1993). Test-taking strategies instruction for adolescents with emotional and behavioral disorders. *Journal of Emotional and Behavioral Disorders, 1,* 188–189.

Schumaker, J. B, & Deshler, D. D. (1992). Validation of learning strategy interventions for students with learning disabilities: Results of a programmatic research effort. In B. Y. L. Wong (Ed.), *Contemporary intervention research in learning disabilities: An international perspective* (pp. 22–46). New York: Springer-Verlag.

PART I
PLANNING
TO
ADAPT

1

Adapting Materials

Little research has been conducted on how to adapt materials effectively or how to implement them effectively with students. Research on how to successfully weave adaptations into the general education curriculum is even more sparse. The few studies that have been conducted in this area indicate:

- the process for determining when materials should be adapted,

- the focus of the adaptation,

- how the adaptation should be implemented with students, and

- how students become informed about the adaptation.

In some cases, making and implementing an effective adaptation can be more time consuming and complex than teaching a student the skills needed to meet a particular demand. Therefore, the process for determining when and how a particular adaptation should be used is as important as the adaptation itself. The following steps for making adaptations were developed after reviewing the research on many of the adaptations presented in this book. These steps provide a suggested framework for making decisions about using material adaptations effectively.

Step 1. Create a Plan for Adapting Materials

Adapting materials is just one part of an overall plan for students with disabilities; to be effective, the adaptations will require sustained development and support. Decisions must be made within the framework of a larger plan that includes consideration of basic and strategic skills instruction and the roles of those involved in the adaptation process (e.g., general education teachers vis à vis special education teachers). In planning for materials adaptations, it is important to:

- Involve your administrator and curriculum or program coordinator from the beginning of the plan.

- Identify exactly who will be responsible for making, implementing, supporting, and evaluating the adaptation over the course of the year. Remember, adaptations that can benefit an entire class or several classes are more likely to be supported and maintained.

- Enlist local business people and parents to assist and support you.

- As much as possible, involve students, clerical staff, counselors, administrators, librarians, volunteers, and paraprofessionals. Everyone plays an important part in making adaptations work in a school.

- Use workshops and other means of dissemination to inform administrators, other teachers, and parents about the different types of adaptations and collaborative models that support students.

The questions in Figure 1 can provide guidance in developing a plan to implement adaptations in your school.[1]

Step 2. Identify and Evaluate the Demands That Students Are Not Meeting

Once a plan is in place, the individuals or team responsible for creating adaptations will need to observe the target students' performances when they are given tasks requiring the use of typical instructional materials. If students have difficulty with a task, different solutions may be required depending on the level of the difficulty. A problem may occur at any or all of the following levels:

Level 1: Acquiring or getting the important information from written materials.

[1]Specific procedures for collaboratively planning and implementing material adaptations are listed in *Collaborative Problem Solving* (Knackendoffel, Robinson, Schumaker, & Deshler, 1992).

FIGURE 1
Questions to Address
in Developing an Implementation Plan

Who

- Who will be responsible for preparing the adaptation?
- Who will be responsible for implementing the adaptation?
- Who is available to help with preparing and implementing the adaptation?
- Who is going to pay for the costs of the adaptation?
- Who will monitor the development and implementation of the adaptation?
- Who will implement the strategy instruction?

What

- What previous responsibilities must the preparer(s) give up in order to add this additional responsibility?
- What resources, space, and equipment will be required for making and implementing the adaptation?
- What is the timeline for implementing and evaluating the adaptation?

Where and When

- Where and when will the adaptation be prepared?
- Where and when will strategy instruction be implemented?

How

- How much time will be required for making the adaptation?
- How will the quality of the adaptation be monitored and evaluated?
- How will the effectiveness of the adaptation be determined?
- How long will strategy instruction take?

Other

- Is this an isolated, one-time adaptation, or is a series of adaptations required?
- Will this adaptation need to be sustained? For how long?
- Should a strategy be taught to students simultaneously with the use of the adaptation?

Level 2: Storing or remembering information presented in materials so that the information can be used at a later date.

Level 3: Expressing information or demonstrating competence on written tests.

For example, if a student has a problem at Level 1, the student probably is not going to be successful at Levels 2 or 3 without intervention at those levels as well. If the problem is at Level 2, the student probably is not going to be successful at Level 3. In other words, some students may need adaptations and/or instruction at all three levels. Thus, once a task has been identified, the level of the task determines the level of the intervention.

Step 3. Develop Goals for Teaching Strategies and Making Adaptations

Once the teacher has pinpointed the problem, he or she will need to decide how it will be addressed. Some problems can be solved by adaptations; other problems may signal the need for intensive instruction in skills or strategies. Frequently, teachers may need to provide adaptations simultaneously with instruction in needed learning strategies.

All adaptations lead students to become dependent on the person who makes them. Therefore, before an adaptation is made for an individual student, educators must decide carefully the best approach to address the student's disability and promote success. Adaptations should be approached as short-term solutions within the context of a long-term plan for teaching skills and strategies that will promote the student's independence as a learner and ultimately reduce the need for the adaptations. The student's instructional goals should reflect this approach.

Step 4. Determine the Need for Content Adaptations versus Format Adaptations

Teachers who make content adaptations also need to meet current local and state education standards. A teacher may consider content adaptation only when the student's individualized education program (IEP) has noted that the curriculum is inappropriate for him or her. In cases in which the curriculum is considered appropriate for the student, adaptations may focus on format, not on content, since content adaptations can affect the fulfillment of curriculum standards. In some cases, the IEP meeting may address the degree to which state standards and assessments can be modified. Based on the outcomes of the IEP meeting, the teacher may need to decide which parts of the curriculum content the student will be required to learn and what will constitute mastery of the important course content.

When content adaptation is neither possible nor desirable, it is still crucial to identify the essential elements of the content (i.e., the critical concepts) that the student must learn. To help you decide what format adaptations should be made, answer the following strategic questions:

1. What are the critical concepts that must be mastered over the course of the year in this subject? (For example: "What are the 10 most important critical concepts that every student should learn in this seventh-grade social studies class?")

2. What type of information must be mastered in each unit to ensure that the course ideas are mastered? (For example: "For each unit in seventh-grade social studies, what five concepts do students need to know and what five questions should they be able to answer about these concepts?")

3. How will students be expected to demonstrate mastery of the critical content in each unit and at the end of the course? (For example: "Students will need to define each concept and provide at least one example of each concept. Students must state [orally or in writing] the essential answer to each of the five unit questions and must answer multiple-choice, matching, and true/false test questions about information related to the five unit questions.")

In cases in which content is judged appropriate for a student, the information about critical concepts should be used as a guide to adapting the format of the curriculum to assist the student in mastering content. Format adaptations are used to enhance or compensate for mismatches between the presentation or design of the materials and the skills and strategies of the student. In format adaptations, the information in the materials is not altered.

Step 5. Identify the Features of the Materials That Need To Be Adapted

The design of materials can create several types of problems for students with disabilities. Many of these problems, some possible short-term adaptation solutions, and some long-term instructional goals associated with the problems are listed in Table 1. Teachers can use this table to help identify features of curricular units and expectations that might be causing a learning problem.

Other resources might be used in this identification process as well. For example, some of the developers of the adaptations included in this book have provided guidelines for identifying features of materials that may be inconsiderate to the learner. Deshler, Schumaker, and McKnight (1997), for instance, have provided a two-page Checklist for Considerate Text Characteristics that a teacher can complete prior to making any textbook adoptions or adaptations (see Appendix, Figure A1). This checklist enables teachers to identify the inconsiderate features of their textbooks; the accompanying list of teacher strategies (Appendix, Figure A2) shows how to compensate for the weak features in the curriculum.

Step 6. Determine the Type of Adaptation That Will Enable the Student To Meet the Demand

Once the materials have been evaluated and possible problem areas have been identified, the type of format adaptation must be selected. Format adaptations can be made by:

1. *Altering existing materials.* Sometimes materials are appropriate but must be modified physically to make them more accessible or more sensitive to learning needs. In this type of adaptation, the teacher rewrites, reorganizes, adds to, or recasts the information in alternate ways so that the student can access regular curriculum material independently. For example, the teacher may prepare an audiotape and a study guide for the student to use as text material is read.

2. *Mediating existing materials.* When learning problems require more support than mere alteration of the existing materials, the teacher can provide additional instructional support, guidance, and direction to students in the use of existing materials. The teacher alters his or her instruction to mediate the barriers presented by the design of the materials. The teacher directly leads students to respond to and interact with existing materials in different ways. For example, the teacher can direct students to survey the reading material to collaboratively preview the text and then have them create an outline of the reading material as a reading and study guide.

TABLE 1
Design Problems in Curriculum Materials and Possible Solutions

Design Problem	Short-Term Design Adaptation	Long-Term Instructional Goal
1. *Abstractness.* The content appears too conceptual, hypothetical, and impractical.	Provide students with more concrete examples, analogies, interpretations, or experiences.	Teach students how to seek more examples, explanations, and interpretations through questioning and research.
2. *Organization.* The organization is not clear or is poorly structured.	Make the organization explicit for students by creating graphic organizers and reading guides and inserting cues that focus attention.	Teach students how to survey materials and identify text organization, read to confirm organization of ideas, and reorganize information for personal understanding and use.
3. *Relevance.* The information does not appear to have any relationship to students or their lives.	Make the connections between the information and students' lives explicit by building rationales and tying information to student experiences.	Teach students to ask appropriate questions about relevance, search for personal connections, and explore ways to make content relevant when given material that appears irrelevant to their lives.
4. *Interest.* The information or presentation of the information is boring.	Present information and assignments in ways that build on students' attention spans, participation, strengths, and interests.	Teach students self-management strategies for controlling attention in boring situations and how to take advantage of options and choices provided in assignments to make work more interesting.
5. *Skills.* The information is written at a level that assumes and requires skills beyond those possessed by students.	Present information in ways that use the skills students have.	Provide intensive instruction in basic skills required for basic literacy to middle-school students who are unprepared for secondary school content.
6. *Strategies.* The information is presented in ways that assume that students know how to approach tasks effectively and efficiently in strategic ways.	Provide instruction in learning strategies to students who do not know how to approach and complete tasks.	Cue and guide students in how to approach and complete learning and performance tasks by leading them through complex tasks.

Design Problem	*Short-Term* *Design Adaptation*	*Long-Term* *Instructional Goal*
7. *Background.* Understanding information usually requires critical background knowledge, but students often lack the experiences and concepts (or cannot make connections to personal background experiences) to make new information meaningful.	Present information in ways that provide background experiences or make background linkages clear.	Teach students how to become consumers of information from a variety of information sources and how to ask questions of these sources to gain background knowledge and insights.
8. *Complexity.* The information or associated tasks have many parts or layers.	Break down the information or tasks and present them explicitly and in different ways so that students can learn and perform.	Teach students how to "chunk" tasks, represent complex information graphically, ask clarifying questions, and work collaboratively in teams to attack complex tasks.
9. *Quantity.* There is a lot of difficult or complex information that is crucial to remember.	Present the information in ways that facilitate remembering.	Teach strategies for chunking, organizing, and remembering information.
10. *Activities.* The instructional activities and sequences provided do not lead to understanding or mastery.	Provide students with scaffolded learning experiences that include additional or alternative instructional activities, activity sequences, or practice experiences to ensure mastery at each level of learning before instruction continues.	Teach students to independently check and redo work, review information, seek help, ask clarifying questions, and inform others when they need more or different types of instruction before instruction in more content begins.
11. *Outcomes.* The information does not cue students how to think about or study information to meet intended outcomes.	Inform students about expectations for their learning and performance.	Teach students how to identify expectations and goals embedded in materials or to create and adjust goals based on previous experiences with similar materials.
12. *Responses.* The material does not provide options for students to demonstrate competence in different ways.	Provide opportunities to students to demonstrate what they know in different ways.	Teach students how they can best demonstrate competence, identify and take advantage of performance options and choices when they are offered, and request appropriate adaptations of tests and competency evaluations.

3. *Selecting alternate materials.* Sometimes the existing materials are so poorly designed that too much time and too many resources would be required to alter or mediate existing materials. When this level of frustration is reached, the format of the existing curriculum may be inappropriate, and a new set of curriculum materials should be selected—materials that are more sensitive to the needs of students with disabilities or that are inherently designed to compensate for many student learning problems. For example, a teacher may use an interactive computer program in science that cues critical ideas, reads text, inserts graphic organizers, defines and illustrates words, presents and reinforces learning in smaller increments, and provides more opportunities for practice and cumulative review—in short, universally designed curricular materials.[2]

Most of the examples described here refer to instructional adaptations, but the same principles apply when making adaptations to written tests. For example:

- Audiotape an existing test or break it down into chunks. (Adapting existing materials.)

- Lead students through an existing test by helping them organize their time, rephrasing test questions, or allowing them to ask questions about test questions. (Mediating existing materials.)

- Obtain interactive CD-ROM software that tests the student through an interactive process and can provide feedback on an ongoing basis. (Selecting alternate materials.)

- Inquire about the types of adaptations that are appropriate for standardized tests used by the school district. Test publishers often provide information about the types of adaptations that were included in the norming of the test and that are allowed.

More Examples

For more ideas on the types of adaptations that work for students with disabilities within the three categories listed here, see the examples of material adaptations that are highlighted in Part II of this volume.

[2]*Editor's note:* While adaptations can be built in to print materials, the extreme flexibility of digital media make them a desirable means to provide such adaptive alternatives as mentioned in the text. For a more complete description of universal design for curriculum access, see the ERIC/OSEP Special Project Topical Brief *A Curriculum Every Student Can Use: Design Principles for Student Access,* available through The Council for Exceptional Children.

These examples are included because research has shown that their use improves the performance of students with disabilities. They are presented as models or springboards for adaptations. Information on obtaining more details is provided at the end of each example.

Step 7. Inform Students and Parents About the Adaptation

Adaptations are more likely to be successful when they are offered and introduced to the student or to the whole class at the beginning of the year. Students should be taught explicit strategies to use any adaptation effectively and how to process the information received through the adaptation. For example, simply providing an audio or video recording of information to a student who cannot read may be an ineffective adaptation of materials. Research has shown that simply listening to audiotaped text does not compensate for poor learning strategies, poorly organized text, or limited background experiences (see p. 35). As students progress, they should be taught how to recognize the need for and request material adaptations. Since adaptations can promote dependence, students should learn to become as independent as possible in profiting from the adaptation.

Parents also should be informed of the types of adaptations that will be provided at the beginning of the year and how they will be implemented. They should be informed of any role that they might play in terms of helping the student use the adaptation. A one-page Policy and Implementation Sheet can inform parents about how they might become involved. Parents can also be informed about adaptations at IEP meetings and parent–teacher conferences. Decisions about content adaptations resulting in the use of alternative curricula should always be made at an IEP meeting. Decisions about format adaptations may be made more informally, but parents will need to be reassured that the content is not being altered and that standards are being met.

Step 8. Implement, Evaluate, and Adjust the Adaptation

Once a student has been taught how to use the adaptation, it should be used systematically. Then instruction should begin with strategies that will gradually increase the student's independence and make the adaptation less necessary.

As the adaptation is implemented, the teacher should evaluate its effect to determine whether or not the desired outcomes are being achieved. For example, if a study guide has been developed to help the student retrieve information from the text, the evaluation should focus on whether the student can now answer the questions about the text correctly. If not, adjustments will be needed in the study guide or in how the student is using the study guide. The use of adaptations should significantly reduce failure and learning difficulties. If an adaptation does not do this, then the previous steps may need to be revisited.

Step 9. Fade the Adaptation When Possible

Adaptations usually are short-term solutions offered to a student to allow classroom learning and participation until the needed skills and strategies can be taught. Once an adaptation is in place, the teacher should begin to plan with other teachers regarding how to teach the needed skills and strategies. Once the student has learned the necessary skills and strategies, the adaptation should be faded. Table 1 (pages 12–13) gives examples of short-term adaptations and long-term instructional goals. The adaptation should not be removed until the student has been taught the required skill or strategy to learn and complete tasks independently. For some students, an adaptation may be required for several months, while for others it may be maintained for years. For still other students, the IEP may indicate that other instructional goals are more important than teaching the independent skills and strategies enabled by the adaptation. For these students, the adaptation may become a permanent accommodation and will be required for high school and in postsecondary life experiences. In a case such as this, the student should be taught how the adaptation is implemented, how to advocate use of the accommodation, and the legal right to accommodations related to his or her disability.

References

Deshler, D. D., Schumaker, J. B., & McKnight, P. C. (1997). *The survey routine.* Lawrence: University of Kansas Press.

Knackendoffel, E. A., Robinson, S., Schumaker, J. B., & Deshler, D. D. (1992). *Collaborative problem solving.* Lawrence, KS: Edge Enterprises.

PART II
EXAMPLES
OF
MATERIAL
ADAPTATIONS

This section contains descriptions of material adaptations that research has found to enhance the performance of middle-school students with disabilities. The adaptations are organized into three groups: (1) altering existing materials, (2) mediating existing materials, and (3) selecting alternate materials. (See Table 2 for a summary of each example.) They are presented here to provide models for the kinds of adaptations that might be made and as springboards for the creative process. Additional information can be obtained about each adaptation by contacting the developers.

TABLE 2
Examples of Material Adaptations

Type 1: Altering Existing Materials

Problem	Solution	Adaptation
Difficulty reading and obtaining information from textbooks that do not consider differing levels of ability.	• A diagnostic/prescriptive procedure for matching students to their highest level of textbook instruction through the use of study questions and text-related tests.	*Title: Differentiated Textbook Instruction* (p. 21) [1] *Author:* Horton *Developers:* Horton, Lovitt, & Christensen *Area:* Across subject areas—Study Guides

Assignments often do not provide sufficient information for successful completion; student questioning or planning is not always encouraged; students are not given options and choices that allow them to build on strengths and interests.	• Procedures that help teachers:
	  – Plan motivating assignments.
	  – Consider learning difficulties.
	  – Teach students how to listen to and explore assignment dimensions and review completed assignments.
	• A planner that prompts students through the assignment completion process.
		Title: The Quality Assignment Routine and The Quality Quest Planner (p. 27) [2] *Author:* Schumaker *Developers:* Rademacher, Schumaker, Deshler, & Lenz; Hughes, Ruhl, Rademacher, Schumaker, & Deshler *Area:* Assignments across subject areas

Difficulty differentiating important information from less important and/or supporting information. Audiotapes using verbatim text do not address the inconsiderate nature of texts and ignore the processing strategies required for good reading.	• A system for coding and audiotaping text:
	  – to make it more user-friendly and
	  – to cue students to read the text strategically for maximum benefit.
		Title: S.O.S: Survey, Obtain Information, Self-Test (p. 34) [3] *Author:* Schumaker *Developers:* Schumaker, Deshler, & Denton *Area:* Textbooks across subject areas

Problem	Solution	Adaptation
Difficulty with the content structure and association of the most important information with tasks and outcomes. Students get lost in the instructional process and are overwhelmed by the amount of content.	• Sets of graphic organizers that help teachers introduce and teach content that is organized into courses, units, and lessons to ensure student attention to and understanding of progress through content learning.	*Title: Content Organizers* (p. 38) **4** *Author:* Lenz *Developers:* Lenz, Schumaker, & Deshler *Area:* Across subject areas
Difficulty identifying key concepts in subject-area materials, linking concepts to prior knowledge, and connecting concepts to other new information.	• A set of graphic organizers that – Draw attention to text-based concepts. – Introduce concepts. – Ensure that concepts are connected to prior knowledge. – Assist students in comparing multiple concepts.	*Title: Concept Organizers* (p. 47) **5** *Author:* Bulgren *Developers:* Bulgren, Schumaker, & Deshler *Area:* Major concepts across subject areas
Difficulty remembering large quantities of information in content classes.	• Procedures for teachers to identify key information in texts and develop and present mnemonic devices for learning and remembering the information.	*Title: Mnemonic Adaptations* (p. 59) **6** *Authors:* Scruggs & Mastropieri *Developers:* Scruggs & Mastropieri *Area:* Mastering information across subject areas
Lack of background knowledge, reading and writing skills, language skills, and test-taking skills; difficulty following directions and understanding abstract ideas associated with performance assessments.	• A sequence of prompts that teachers can use to guide students to think critically about the problem, solve it, and express that solution in a way that demonstrates competence in the area.	*Title: Problem-Solving Prompts for Performance Assessments* (p. 67) **7** *Author:* Tindal *Developers:* Tindal & McCleery *Area:* Performance assessments across subject areas
Lack of reading skills or strategies for gaining information out of textbooks and other written materials.	• A set of procedures to evaluate reading materials. • The teacher then leads students through an interactive process to create a prereading guide which they then use to complete the reading assignment.	*Title: The Survey Routine* (p. 74) **8** *Author:* Schumaker *Developers:* Deshler, Schumaker, & McKnight *Area:* Textbooks across subject areas

continues

TABLE 2 *(Continued)*

Type 3: Selecting Alternate Materials

Problem	Solution	Adaptation
Difficulty differentiating important information from less important and/or supporting information and identifying big ideas within text.	• An alternative textbook for general education classrooms in which the arrangement of content promotes understanding of big ideas.	*Title: Coherent Text Built Around Big Ideas* [9] (p. 87) *Author:* Grossen *Developers:* Carnine, Crawford, Harniss, & Hollenbeck *Area:* U.S. history
Lack of basic skills necessary to profit from inquiry- or discovery-based materials.	• A reasoning and writing program with built-in adaptations for students with disabilities. Thinking processes are made explicit through structured instruction.	*Title: Reasoning and Writing* (p. 93) [10] *Author:* Grossen *Developers:* Engelmann, Silbert, & Grossen *Area:* Reasoning
Difficulty reading complex science materials; lack of background knowledge for understanding science concepts; no opportunities for frequent comprehension checks; difficulty learning approaches for learning science.	• A videodisc curriculum with built-in adaptations based on principles of instructional design that are sensitive to the needs of students with disabilities. • The videodisc presents information and activities that ensure student comprehension, interaction, and mastery.	*Title: Science Videodisc Media* (p. 98) [11] *Author:* Grossen *Developers:* Engelmann, Hofmeister, & Carnine *Area:* Science
Many approaches to math instruction do not provide the supports and checks to promote math competence.	• Math programs with built-in adaptations for students with disabilities.	*Titles: Connecting Math Concepts, SRA, and Core Concepts Videodisc Programs* (p. 105) [12] *Author:* Grossen *Developers:* Engelmann, S., Carnine, Engelmann, O., & Kelly; Engelmann, S., Hofmeister, & Carnine *Area:* Mathematics

2

Adapting Existing Materials

This chapter discusses the following adaptations:

1. Differentiated Textbook Instruction *(Horton, Lovitt, & Christensen).*

2. The Quality Assignment Routine *(Rademacher, Schumaker, Deshler, & Lenz) and The Quality Quest Planner (Hughes, Ruhl, Rademacher, Schumaker, & Deshler).*

3. S.O.S.: Survey, Obtain Information, Self-Test *(Schumaker, Deshler, & Denton).*

The adaptation of existing materials is used when the materials are judged to be appropriate but need some simple modifications to make them more accessible. Existing materials are physically changed so that they are more sensitive to learning needs. You can either rewrite, reorganize, add to, or recast the information in alternate ways so that the student can access regular curriculum material independently. For example, you can prepare an audiotape and study guide for the student to use as text material is read.

1. Differentiated Textbook Instruction

Because of poor reading and study skills, many middle school students with learning disabilities or who are otherwise low-achieving students are unable to read their assigned textbooks with the proficiency required to abstract new information and assimilate that information with previously learned material (Deshler, 1978; Horton & Lovitt, 1994; Torgeson, 1985; Zigmond, Vallecorsa, & Leinhardt, 1980).[1] The problem is exacerbated by a host of "inconsiderate" features of many textbooks, including:

- Complex syntactical structures.

- Esoteric vocabularies.

- Heavy information loads.

- Dense concentrations of novel concepts (Armbruster, 1984; Tyree, Fiore, & Cook, 1994).

Unlike facile readers, who may be able to comprehend a variety of textual material through independent reading and study, less skilled readers require adaptive techniques to manage the large number of ideas and facts presented in many textbooks.

The Adaptation

In this adaptation, you can apply the following diagnostic-prescriptive approach to individualizing textbook instruction if you:

1. Select various passages from the textbook, construct study guides and tests for those passages, then have students read the selected passages and complete the study guides independently prior to formally beginning instruction.

2. Use the diagnostic information to place students into one of three instructional groups: teacher-directed, dyadic (paired), or independent.

3. Implement subsequent textbook instruction differently for each group.

[1]Research conducted at the University of Washington has shown that wide variation exists in students' ability to read and understand content-area textbooks among middle-school students classified as learning disabled and nondisabled pupils. For example, when students with learning disabilities read textbooks in inclusive secondary programs, their oral reading rates ranged from 32 to 152 words per minute (Lovitt, Horton, & Bergerud, 1987).

Diagnostic Procedure

You can follow these steps to diagnose students' highest level of independent activity with their assigned textbook:

1. Choose two passages from the textbook of approximately 1,200 words each that contain information to be covered in class.

2. Create a 15-item study guide drawing information from the beginning, middle, and end of each passage. (The study guide is a worksheet consisting of questions that isolate important facts and concepts from critical passages in the text that contain the core of information you will teach and that are difficult for students.)

3. For each study guide, create a 15-item multiple-choice test, each question having four choices. The test should have 12 questions written at the factual level and directly corresponding to 12 items on the study guide and 3 questions written at the interpretive level (students must combine information from more than one part of the passage or infer beyond the passage).

4. Before formally beginning instruction, in two separate class sessions, give students 12 minutes to read the passage, 20 minutes to complete the study guide independently, and up to 20 minutes to complete the multiple-choice test.

Placing Students in Three Instructional Groups

Once the diagnostic tests are given, individualize your textbook instruction by doing the following:

1. Calculate an average score for each student based on the scores the student earned on the two diagnostic tests.

2. Assign students to the three instructional groups, using the following criteria based on their scores: 0%–47%, teacher directed; 53%–73%, paired group; 80%–100%, independent study.

The study guides you prepare for the teacher-directed group should contain paragraph and page references after each question as an aid to locating the answers in the passage. The guides for the dyadic group should contain a page number reference only after each question. The guides for the independent students should contain no referential cues. (See Figure 2.) Prepare 15-item multiple-choice tests as described earlier.

FIGURE 2
Study Guide Information*

Teacher-Directed Group:
Why is Simon Bolivar honored throughout the world? Page 145, paragraph 3.

Dyadic Group:
Why is Simon Bolivar honored throughout the world? Page 145

Independent Group:
Why is Simon Bolivar honored throughout the world?

Answer:
He led many important battles between 1810 and 1824, and he liberated five South American countries.

* This is how the same item of information appeared on the three types of study guides for a seventh-grade social studies text on the history of Latin America and Canada. The three descriptive group names are not shown on the students' guides, nor is the answer provided on their sheets.

Implementing Three Instructional Groups Simultaneously

Three instructional groups can be implemented by means of the following procedure:

1. All students read a 1,200-word passage of text independently for 12 minutes.

2. Students divide into three instructional groups and complete the study guide for 20 minutes, using their textbooks. The teacher-directed students are seated in a row on one side of the classroom; the dyadic students are seated in two rows on the opposite side of the classroom with their desks pulled together in pairs; and the independent students are seated in a row in the middle of the classroom. Lead the teacher-directed students in completing and studying the guide questions as a group. Have the dyadic students work in pairs, based on compatibility, to complete the study guide questions by cooperatively answering the questions on an item-by-item basis, followed by quizzing each other. The independent students will complete and study the guides independently.

3. Have the students take the 15-item, closed-book, multiple-choice test. Read aloud the test questions and the choices for the teacher-directed group, while the others work on their own.

What Research Backs It Up?

This diagnostic-prescriptive approach to matching students to their highest level of independent activity with textbooks was scientifically validated with seventh-grade students—some of whom had learning disabilities—in physical science and social studies classes, as well as with tenth-grade students in life science and American history—all of whom were classified as having learning disabilities or as needing remedial instruction (Horton, Lovitt, & Christensen, 1991). Four classes of students were given the diagnostic measures as described. The number of students in teacher-directed groups ranged from five to nine across classes, and each teacher-directed group contained some students who were classified as having learning disabilities and some who were not. One student at the middle school level and four high school students with learning disabilities were placed in the dyadic or independent groups.

The results of this study indicated that when students were randomly assigned to six occasions in which they were presented a study guide that they completed independently and six occasions in which they were placed in one of the three instructional groups to complete the guides and tests as described, in 87% of the cases, mean scores were higher in the adapted multilevel study guide treatment on factual test items. Of the 12 students with learning disabilities who were placed in teacher-directed groups across classes in the study, 10 scored significantly higher on factual questions as a result of the adapted multilevel diagnostic-prescriptive approach to textbook instruction than when they studied the guide independently.

What Does It Look Like in Practice?

Ben was enrolled in Mrs. Whitacre's seventh-grade social studies class. This was a two-semester class covering the history of Latin America and Canada and using a textbook written at the ninth-grade level. Based on the information gained from administering the diagnostic measures described earlier (i.e., two reading passages, study guides, and tests), Mrs. Whitacre anticipated that the course would be difficult for Ben because he earned an average score of 28%. Additionally, Ben's records indicated that he had a learning disability that was specifically manifested in poor reading comprehension. His standardized test scores indicated that he was reading at the third-grade level. To address this issue, Mrs. Whitacre placed Ben in the teacher-directed group and followed the procedures for implementing instruction for that group, while monitoring the instruction of the dyadic and independent groups at the same time.

Over the course of the school year, Ben averaged 74% on tests for the first semester and 82% on tests taken during the second semester. Moreover, during the second semester, Ben asked whether he could try working in the dyadic group, and after he became familiar with the procedure, he maintained his performance on tests at the same level as he had achieved when he was participating in the teacher-directed group.

Who Can Provide Additional Information?

Steve Horton
16105 NE 106th Street
Redmond, WA 98052
425/881-7860

What Additional Information Is Available?

Horton, S. V., Lovitt, T. C., & Christensen, C. (1991). Matching three classifications of secondary students to differential levels of study guides. *Journal of Learning Disabilities, 24,* 518–529.

References

Armbruster, B. B. (1984). The problem of "inconsiderate text." In G. G. Duffy, L. R. Roehler, & J. Mason (Eds.), *Comprehension instruction: Perspectives and suggestions* (pp. 202–217). New York: Longman.

Deshler, D. D. (1978). Psychoeducational aspects of learning disabled adolescents. In L. Mann, L. Goodman, & J. L. Wiederholt (Eds.), *Teaching the learning-disabled adolescent* (pp. 47–74). Boston: Houghton Mifflin.

Horton, S. V., & Lovitt, T. C. (1994). A comparison of two methods of administering group reading inventories to diverse learners: Computer versus pencil and paper. *Remedial and Special Education, 13,* 378–390.

Horton, S. V., Lovitt, T. C., & Christensen, C. (1991). Matching three classifications of secondary students to differential levels of study guides. *Journal of Learning Disabilities, 24,* 518–529.

Lovitt, T. C., Horton, S. V., & Bergerud, D. (1987). Matching students with textbooks: An alternative to readability formulas and standardized tests. *British Columbia Journal of Special Education, 2*(1), 49–55.

Torgeson, J. K. (1985). Memory processes in reading disabled children. *Journal of Learning Disabilities, 18,* 350–357.

Tyree, R. B., Fiore, T. A., & Cook, R. A. (1994). Instructional materials for diverse learners. Features and considerations for textbook design. *Remedial and Special Education, 15,* 363–374.

Zigmond, N., Vallecorsa, A., & Leinhardt, O. (1980). Reading instruction for students with learning disabilities. *Topics in Language Disorders, 1,* 89–98.

2. The Quality Assignment Routine and The Quality Quest Planner

At the middle school level, students are expected to record each homework assignment in writing, take the necessary materials home, complete the assignment at home, return the materials to the school, and hand the assignment in on time. Although this multistep process is formidable enough for students with disabilities, it becomes even more difficult when all the students in the class are expected to complete the same assignment in the same way and individual differences and preferences are not taken into account. In addition, even when content adaptations are specified on an IEP, assignments do not always reflect their modified expectations. As a result, students with disabilities often do not complete their homework assignments. This two-part adaptation was developed to be useful across subject-matter areas to help you plan and present assignments that all students in the class can complete as well as to help students record and complete the assignments.

The Adaptation

In the first part of this adaptation, you can adapt the assignment to fit the skills and needs of the students in the class. Next, as you present the assignment to students using a visual display, they will record the assignment in a special assignment planner that contains prompts for completing all the steps in the assignment-completion process.

In the first part, the Quality Assignment Routine (Rademacher, Deshler, Schumaker, & Lenz, 1998) helps you plan, present, and evaluate the assignment. A special worksheet prompts you to consider the following:

FIGURE 3
Assignment Window

SUBJECT _English_____ DATE: GIVEN _5/4_ DUE _5/5_ TURNED IN ____ ☐

Read	_Answer_	(_Write_)	_Other_

D: Define 5 vocab. wds., p. 67. Write meaningful sentence/ea.

O: Choose which 5 words

G: 1. spell vocab. wds. correctly, 2. underline wds. Worth: 20 pts

S/R: Text; glossary

Parts: 1. Pick wds   5 min   # of study sessions: ___2___ Actual Grade Received:

____2. Defins/exps 45 min Grade Goal: Ⓐᵇ Bᵃ Cᵃ ____ A B C D F

____3. Check   10 min Quality Goal: Ⓐᵇ Bᵃ Cᵃ   Other: _____

Goal: Use COPS.

- The purpose of the assignment.

- Its relevance to students.

- Student choices for completing the assignment that take into account their skills. For example, students might choose a book to be read for a book report so that it will be at their readability level. For the "report" they could draw an ad, create a test complete with an answer key, create several pictures of scenery, or make a poster.

- Problems students might encounter completing the assignment.

- Solutions to those problems that can be explained to the students.

The worksheet also helps you to plan clear directions for the assignment, supplies and resources that might need to be made available, and the grading criteria for the assignment.

Next, you plan how this information will be visually displayed for the students. For simple assignments, a graphic device called the _Assignment Window_ is used (see Figure 3). For complex assignments, an _Assignment Handout_ is created (see Figure 4).

FIGURE 4

ASSIGNMENT HANDOUT

World History
March 12, 1997

Assignment: Journal on Ancient Greece
Date due: March 18
Points: 100 points (1/10 of unit grade)
Purpose: So we can analyze why such a highly developed civilization fell apart, and prevent the same thing from happening to our own civilization.

Directions: Choose some aspect of Greek culture that interests you (e.g., sports, politics, art, drama, music, domestic life). Focusing on that interest, create a journal that describes that aspect of life for someone who lived in Ancient Greece and had that same interest. Show one good thing and one bad about that aspect of culture.

Options:
1. You may do this assignment either by yourself or with a partner.
2. Journal may be either a written diary or an audiotape.
3. Choose whether the person you're writing for lived in Athens or Sparta.

Grading Criteria:
1. Journal must have at least seven entries. Each entry must have a date. Entries need not be consecutive (e.g., doesn't have to be March 1, 2, 3; can be Mar. 1, April 2, May 10).
2. Each entry must include at least three statements or sentences.
3. The journal should focus on one good and one bad thing about the interest you have chosen.

Supplies/Resources: Class notes, textbooks, library books, magazine articles, movies, and imaginations.

Then you present the assignment in class, referring students to the information on the Assignment Handout or Window and giving them time to plan how they will complete the assignment. Students record basic information in their Quality Quest Planners, assignment planners specifically designed for students who have difficulty with writing tasks, scheduling time, and completing assignments (Hughes, Ruhl, Rademacher, Schumaker, & Deshler, 1995). Within the planner are Assignment Windows similar to the visual display you would use to present the assignment, as well as monthly and weekly calendars for scheduling work time. Words and boxes throughout the planner prompt students through the assignment-completion process.

Finally, in grading the assignment, you use a special visual display to indicate to students the requirements that were met and those that were not met.

What Research Backs It Up?

Research was conducted to develop and validate these adaptations. First, focus group sessions were held with middle school students and teachers to have them identify the elements that should comprise the Quality Assignment Routine. Second, the identified elements were validated by groups of teachers, students with disabilities, and other students. Third, a study was conducted to determine whether teachers could and would use the routine in their classes (Rademacher, 1993).

Six secondary general education teachers learned to plan, explain, and evaluate student assignments during a workshop. Results showed that teachers who received the training and incorporated these planning, presentation, and evaluation procedures into their routines were significantly more satisfied with assignments and assignment outcomes (as were their students) than teachers who did not receive the training and their students (Rademacher, Schumaker, & Deshler, 1996).

The adapted planner was validated in a separate study (Hughes, Ruhl, Schumaker, & Deshler, 1999) that focused on nine middle-school students in grades six through eight who had learning disabilities. Once these students learned how to use the planner and the steps in the assignment-completion process, eight of the nine students' on-time assignment completion rates rose from a mean of 54% to a mean of 77%. The ninth student made no gains. When interviewed, the students indicated that the major reason for not completing an assignment was that they had trouble getting started on assignments. They stated that they now knew and understood what they were to do when they were given an assignment.

What Does It Look Like in Practice?

Mrs. Berry, a seventh-grade English teacher, wanted her students to have lots of practice reading throughout the school year. She decided to require them to read a book every other month, but she was aware

FIGURE 5

Assignment Window

SUBJECT: **English**	DATE: GIVEN_____	DUE____	TURNED IN____	☐

Read	*Answer*	*Write*	*Other*

Monthly book report. See handout.

Parts:_____

_____

_____

Goal:

\# of study sessions: _____

Grade Goal: A☐ B☐ C☐ _

Quality Goal: A☐ B☐ C☐

Actual Grade Received:

A B C D F

Other: _____

---

that the reading skills of her students ranged from third-grade to ninth-grade levels. For example, she knew that Candy Schuler was reading at the fourth-grade level. She also knew that Candy had a very difficult time writing more than a sentence but that she was a talented artist.

Mrs. Berry used the Quality Assignment Planning Sheet to plan the book report assignment that she wanted students to complete monthly. As she thought about the assignment, she realized that her main goal was that the students read regularly and build their reading skills. Thus, as she planned, she built in many options the students could choose among, and she considered how she might work with the special education teachers to ensure that each student would choose books appropriate to his or her reading level. Then she created an Assignment Window and a handout to which the students could refer as they worked on the assignment each month (see Figures 5 and 6). She also created a list of appropriate books organized in categories according to topic and listed by difficulty level, with the easiest books listed first in each category. She presented the assignment to the students after visually displaying the Assignment Window on an overhead transparency and giving each student a handout and a book list.

Candy wrote the assignment in her planner, and when she next met with her special education teacher, the teacher reviewed the

FIGURE 6

ASSIGNMENT HANDOUT

English
Fall '98 Semester

Assignment: Book report
Date due: 1st Friday of every month
Points: 50 points
Purpose: To become a fluent reader.

Directions: Choose a book from the attached book list or ask me for approval of a book. Read the book and create a report using one of the options below.

Options:
1. Create a one-page written summary of book.
2. Create a radio commercial for the book on audiotape.
3. Create a visual advertisement for the book.
4. Design a front and back cover for the book.
5. Create a written test and answer key for the book.

Grading Criteria:
1. Include title and author of book.
2. Describe or show the basic theme of the book.
3. Describe or show the best feature of the book.

Supplies/Resources: Book list, paper, poster board, colored pencils and markers, tape recorder and cassette.

assignment that she had written in her planner and helped her find a book on the list that was appropriate for her reading level. Once she had the book, Candy planned how many pages she would read each day and scheduled time for doing that on the weekly schedules in her

planner. She also chose the kind of book report she would complete. She decided to draw scenery for six scenes in the book for her first report. Candy read the book, completed the drawings, and received an A on the assignment.

Who Can Provide Additional Information?

Coordinator of Training
Center for Research on Learning
University of Kansas
3061 Dole Center
Lawrence, KS 66045
785/864-4780
Website: www.ku-crl.org

What Other Information Is Available?

Hughes, C. A., Ruhl, K. L., Deshler, D. D., & Schumaker, J. B. (1995). *The Assignment Completion Strategy.* Lawrence, KS: Edge Enterprises.

Hughes, C. A., Ruhl, K. L., Rademacher, J., Schumaker, J. B., & Deshler, D. D. (1995). *The Quality Quest Planner.* Lawrence, KS: Edge Enterprises.

Rademacher, J., Deshler, D., Schumaker, J. B., & Lenz, K. (1998). *The Quality Assignment Routine.* Lawrence, KS: Edge Enterprises.

References

Hughes, C. A., Ruhl, K. L., Deshler, D. D., & Schumaker, J. B. (1995). *The Assignment Completion Strategy.* Lawrence, KS: Edge Enterprises.

Hughes, C. A., Ruhl, K. L., Schumaker, J. B., & Deshler, D. D. (1999). *Effects of instruction in an Assignment Completion Strategy on middle-school students' homework completion.* Manuscript in preparation.

Rademacher, J. (1993). *The development and validation of a classroom assignment routine for mainstream settings.* Unpublished doctoral dissertation, University of Kansas, Lawrence.

Rademacher, J., Deshler, D., Schumaker, J. B., & Lenz, K. (1998). *The quality assignment routine.* Lawrence, KS: Edge Enterprises.

Rademacher, J., Schumaker, J. B., & Deshler, D. D. (1996). Development and validation of a classroom assignment routine for inclusive settings. *Learning Disability Quarterly, 19,* 163–178.

3. S.O.S.: Survey, Obtain Information, Self-Test

The problems encountered by students with disabilities in the middle grades are often magnified by the heavy emphasis on reading assignments as a means of acquiring subject-matter information. Often, teachers present major ideas during class and ask students to read supporting material in their textbooks. The readability levels of textbooks are typically at grade level or above, or they vary within the same book. Thus, students who are reading below grade level often do not complete the reading assignments and other related assignments in their subject-matter courses (e.g., social studies, science, English, civics, math). Although the verbatim tape recording of textbooks has been recommended (Hartwell, Wiseman, & Van Reusen, 1979; Mosby, 1980), research has shown that it does not help students learn or improve their performance (Schumaker, Deshler, & Denton, 1984). This adaptation was developed to be useful across subject-matter areas to overcome the shortcomings of traditional audiotaping practices.

The Adaptation

The adaptation involves a specially marked textbook, an audiotape and tape recorder, a study guide, and a set of procedures students use to listen to the audiotape and learn the information in each chapter. As students listen to the audiotape, they participate in three activities: Survey, Obtain Information, and Self-Test (S.O.S.).

During the Survey, students become familiar with the main ideas and organization of the chapter. The textbook/tape contains information regarding the title of the chapter, the relationship of the current chapter to the preceding and following chapters, the introduction of the chapter, the main ideas of the chapter, and the summary. The voice on the tape provides instructions to students to help them find the important information in the chapter and make a skeletal outline of the chapter's main headings. Thus, the voice on the tape acts as a mediator between the students and the textbook information.

As students Obtain Information, they follow along through the chapter while simultaneously listening to the voice on the tape read the most important subheadings and related information and instruct them on what information they are to enter into the skeletal outline as they work through the chapter. Once the outline is complete, students paraphrase their notes to themselves. If they cannot paraphrase their notes, they review the pertinent part of the tape again until they can.

During the Self-Test, students ask themselves the questions on the study guide and answer them, using their notes for reference. If an answer cannot be found in the notes, students review the textbook and the audiotape until the answer is found. The self-testing process continues until the students know all the answers to questions in the study guide.

What Research Backs It Up?

This method was empirically validated with eighth- and tenth-grade students with learning disabilities. The eighth-graders were enrolled in American history classes, and their textbooks were written at the ninth- and tenth-grade levels. Their reading comprehension scores ranged from fourth- to fifth-grade levels. When the eighth-graders read their textbook on their own, they received an average score of 49% on their classroom unit tests. (Tests were publisher-made tests associated with the textbooks and were administered in the general education class.) Thereafter, students listened to S.O.S. tapes for some of their chapters and to verbatim tapes for other chapters for the remainder of the school year. When the students listened to a verbatim tape of the textbook chapter (the voice on the tape read every word in the chapter), their average score on a chapter test was 45%. When they used the adapted tape and S.O.S. procedures, their average score on chapter tests was 87%.

What Does It Look Like in Practice?

Luke was an eighth-grader enrolled in a general education American history course. He was reading at the fourth-grade level, and his textbook was written at the tenth-grade level. Thus, there was a 6-year performance gap between how well he could read and what he was expected to read. His history teacher, Janice Helene, reviewed his first two chapter test scores (both around 50%) and realized that Luke and other students like him would not be able to acquire information by reading the text. She asked two parent volunteers to work with her to prepare coded textbooks and audiotapes for the students. Study guides were already available through the publisher. Once the first chapter was coded and the audiotape produced, she set up a check-out procedure for students so that they could take the books and audiotapes home to complete their reading assignments. She and the special education teacher met with parents to explain the procedure and to ensure that each student had access to a tape player. The special education teacher met with the students during their time in the resource room to instruct them in how to use the coded textbook and tapes.

After learning how to use the tapes, Luke regularly earned As and Bs on his chapter tests.

Who Can Provide Additional Information?

Coordinator of Training
Center for Research on Learning
University of Kansas
3061 Dole Center
Lawrence, KS 66045
785/864-4780
Website: www.ku-crl.org

What Other Information Is Available?

Schumaker, J. B., Deshler, D. D., & Denton, P. H. (1984). An integrated system for providing content to learning disabled adolescents using an audio-taped format. In W. M. Cruickshank & J. M. Kliebhan (Eds.), *Early adolescence to early adulthood: Volume 5, The best of ACLD* (pp. 79–107). Syracuse, NY: Syracuse University Press.

References

Hartwell, L. K., Wiseman, D. E., & VanReusen, A. (1979). Modifying course content for mildly handicapped students at the secondary level. *TEACHING Exceptional Children, 12*(1) 28–32.

Mosby, R. (1980). The application of the developmental by-pass procedure to LD adolescents. *Journal of Learning Disabilities, 13*(7), 21–27.

Schumaker, J. B., Deshler, D. D., & Denton, P. H. (1984). An integrated system for providing content to learning disabled adolescents using an audio-taped format. In W. M. Cruickshank & J. M. Kliebhan (Eds.), *Early adolescence to early adulthood: Volume 5, The best of ACLD* (pp. 79–107). Syracuse, NY: Syracuse University Press.

3

Mediating Existing Materials

The following adaptations are discussed in this chapter:

4. **Content Organizers** *(Lenz, Schumaker, & Deshler).*

5. **Concept Organizers** *(Bulgren, Schumaker, & Lenz).*

6. **Mnemonic Adaptations** *(Scruggs & Mastropieri).*

7. **Problem-Solving Prompts for Performance Assessments** *(Tindal & McCleery).*

8. **The Survey Routine** *(Deshler, Schumaker, & McKnight).*

The adaptation known as *mediating existing materials* is used when students' learning problems require more than alteration of the existing materials. The teacher provides additional instructional support, guidance, and direction to students in the use of existing materials. He or she alters instruction to reduce the barriers presented by the design of the materials and directly leads students to act on and interact with the existing materials in different ways. For example, a teacher may lead students through a survey of the reading material to collaboratively preview the text and then create an outline to serve as a reading and study guide.

---

4. Content Organizers

Because they lack effective strategies to help them focus on, organize, and integrate information, students with disabilities frequently are at a disadvantage when expected to acquire subject-matter information during a course, unit, or lesson. Specifically, students usually have difficulty:

- Relating new information to what they have experienced and learned.

- Seeing the critical ideas among the details.

- Translating the critical ideas into words, phrases, and concepts that make sense to them.

- Identifying how the information is structured.

- Seeing the relationships between different sets of information.

- Generating questions to help focus their attention.

- Projecting and managing time in order to complete tasks.

- Keeping the critical ideas and overall structure of the information in mind as they pass through a course, unit, or lesson.

To address this difficulty, you can adapt the content in ways that will compensate for the lack of these strategies. Content enhancement organizers were developed to help teachers launch a course, unit, or lesson and to provide a framework for ensuring student attention and comprehension throughout the period of instruction.

The Adaptation

To use this adaptation, you prepare a graphic organizer to introduce and teach the content while eliciting a high degree of involvement from students. The organizer contains information that makes explicit both the structure/organization of the content and your intentions for learning. Content organizers can be prepared to introduce lessons, units, or courses. Regardless of the level of instruction, the organizer guides students in recording information graphically to help them answer the following types of questions:

- *Context:* How does the current lesson, unit, or course fit in with what I have learned in the past and what I will learn in the future?

- *Structure:* How is the information organized? How could I explain the critical parts of this information to someone?

- *Thinking:* What relationships (e.g., cause/effect, compare/contrast) are important for understanding? What learning strategies do I need to be using?

- *Questions:* What critical questions do I need to answer to show that I understand the information?

- *Expectations:* What activities, tasks, assignments, or work needs to be done to understand the context, structure, and relationships and to answer the critical questions?

You must take certain steps for students to benefit from the use of content organizers:

1. Select a graphic organizer form that will be used throughout the year.

2. Introduce the form, explain it, and show students how the form will be used.

3. Use the form repeatedly throughout the year to promote student familiarity and usability. Although a draft of the organizer is to be prepared prior to instruction, the final version of the organizer will be constructed interactively and collaboratively with students in class.

4. Ask the students to keep their organizers in notebooks and to be prepared to retrieve them for regular classroom use and for study in other settings.

5. Cue the use of the organizer when it will enlist the participation of students in discussing and recording information; after the organizer has been used, cue it to review learning and how it can be employed for independent study.

The Lesson Organizer, depicted in Figure 7, shows how one teacher and her students approached a lesson on plot for language arts class. Through the construction and presentation of this organizer, the teacher announced the name of the lesson *Plot*, showed and discussed with students how the lesson fit within the broader unit of *Short Story*, and listed and discussed the types of relationships that would be investigated and the types of learning strategies that would be practiced and reinforced.

FIGURE 7
Lesson Organizer

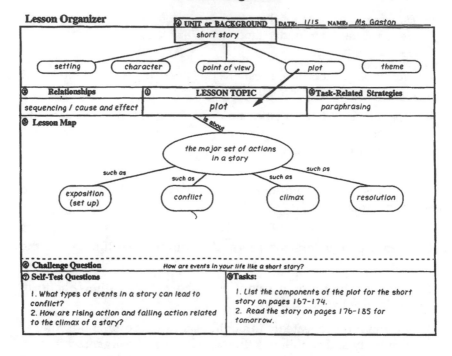

The structure for learning was revealed in the content map of the lesson. The map consisted of a set of shapes connected by lines with labels to show students what content was to be learned. The teacher also posed a challenge question to personalize and create a context for learning. Finally, to provide focus, the teacher and students discussed, generated, and listed a few critical self-test questions that students could use to check understanding, and then listed the tasks that would need to be completed to promote learning. During the lesson, the teacher used the content map to keep students' attention and expanded on each section by adding key vocabulary to the map. The teacher also referred to the listed relationships, learning strategy, and self-test questions throughout the lesson.

The Unit Organizer, depicted in Figure 8, demonstrates how a math teacher and his students approached a unit on decimals. The top of the organizer was used to discuss the relationships between the previous, current, and upcoming units and how the units fit in with the overall content and ideas in the course. Similar to the shapes, lines, and labels in the Lesson Organizer, the unit content map shows how the information about decimals in this unit is organized. Important unit relation-

FIGURE 8
Unit Organizer

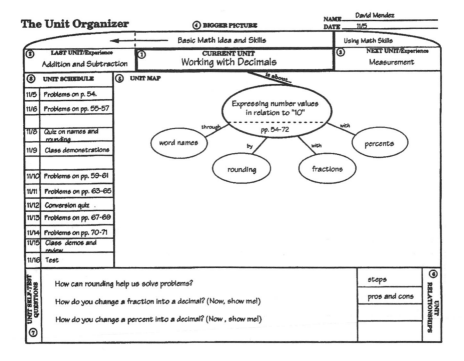

ships and self-test questions are listed at the bottom. Assignments for work in the unit are listed in a Unit Schedule on the left side of the form.

During the unit, the back of the form is used to expand the basic unit content map structure with details, examples, and key words from lessons. This expanded unit map is used throughout the unit to summarize the progress and revisit self-test questions and important unit relationships. The Unit Organizer can be used in conjunction with or in place of Lesson Organizers.

The Course Organizer, depicted in Figures 9 and 10, shows the graphic organizer used to introduce a course in history. On the first page of the Course Organizer (Figure 9), the teacher paraphrased the central idea of the course and provided 10 overarching critical questions that represented the critical course content. These questions were created using state and district frameworks, and students were told that the questions would be used to guide coursework and assessments. Students were also presented with course standards for grading and a progress chart on which they could record scores earned in each unit as the year progressed.

FIGURE 9

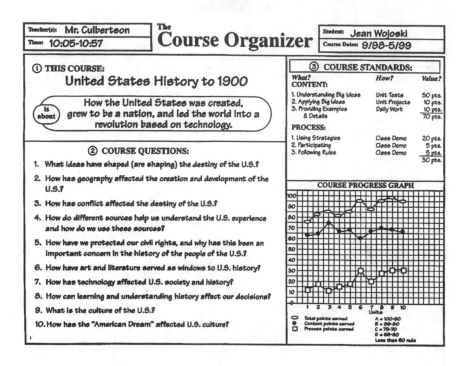

| Teacher(s): Mr. Culbertson | The | Student: Jean Wojoski |
| Time: 10:05-10:57 | **Course Organizer** | Course Dates: 9/98-5/99 |

① **THIS COURSE:**

United States History to 1900

(is about) How the United States was created, grew to be a nation, and led the world into a revolution based on technology.

② **COURSE QUESTIONS:**

1. What ideas have shaped (are shaping) the destiny of the U.S.?
2. How has geography affected the creation and development of the U.S.?
3. How has conflict affected the destiny of the U.S.?
4. How do different sources help us understand the U.S. experience and how do we use these sources?
5. How have we protected our civil rights, and why has this been an important concern in the history of the people of the U.S.?
6. How have art and literature served as windows to U.S. history?
7. How has technology affected U.S. society and history?
8. How can learning and understanding history affect our decisions?
9. What is the culture of the U.S.?
10. How has the "American Dream" affected U.S. culture?

③ **COURSE STANDARDS:**

What?	How?	Value?
CONTENT:		
1. Understanding Big Ideas	Unit Tests	50 pts.
2. Applying Big Ideas	Unit Projects	10 pts.
3. Providing Examples & Details	Daily Work	10 pts.
		70 pts.
PROCESS:		
1. Using Strategies	Class Demo	20 pts.
2. Participating	Class Demo	5 pts.
3. Following Rules	Class Demo	5 pts.
		30 pts.

COURSE PROGRESS GRAPH

Units

○ Total points earned   A = 100-90
● Content points earned   B = 89-80
□ Process points earned   C = 79-70
   D = 69-60
   Less than 60 redo

On the bottom of the second page of the Course Organizer (Figure 10), the teacher drew a map of the units included in the course. As the course progressed, the map was used to review content and discuss relationships between units. At the top of the second page, the teacher presented course rituals (e.g., specific teaching routines and learning strategies) that would be used throughout the year, community principles to be upheld, and the performance options or adaptations to be used for promoting student learning. After each unit, the teacher and class returned to the course organizer and discussed progress in learning course content and creating a successful learning community. The course questions were reviewed and answered regularly, and classroom expectations and processes were evaluated and modified.

Across all three of these content organizers, the organizer and the process used by the teachers to present them can help mediate learning in ways that address learning difficulties. The areas addressed by the organizers focus on controlling attention and facilitating information processing. Finally, teacher guidance in leading students to use the organizer ensures that comprehension is facilitated and reinforced through oral, visual, and interactive learning.

FIGURE 10

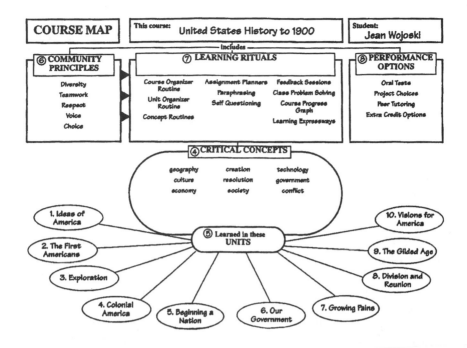

What Research Backs It Up?

Content organizers have been validated through a variety of studies conducted across general education middle school and secondary school classrooms containing students with learning disabilities. An initial study validated the usefulness of advance organizers embedded at the beginning of lessons (Lenz, Alley, & Schumaker, 1987). Data showed that, for students with learning disabilities, learning increased during group instruction only when (a) students were taught how to record information in the advance organizer and use that information to promote learning and (b) the teacher explicitly referred to and used the organizer to guide teaching.

A subsequent study validated the use of graphic organizers to introduce units and coordinate associated lessons (Lenz, Bulgren, Schumaker, Deshler, & Boudah, 1994). In this study, unit test scores of students with disabilities in the classes of teachers who used the Unit Organizer increased, and there was a more direct match between what the teachers and students indicated was important. The long-term and consistent use of the organizers was found to enhance benefits to students.

Finally, the usefulness of organizers for launching and maintaining ideas associated with courses was investigated in a third study (Lenz et al., 1994). In this study, students in experimental classrooms answered more critical course questions than those in comparison classrooms. When a Course Organizer was used and maintained throughout the year, teachers in the experimental classrooms also were more likely to use specific adaptations to promote more inclusive teaching over teachers in comparison classrooms.

What Does It look Like in Practice?

Mr. Kylo, the special education teacher, was scheduled to coteach eighth-grade general science with Ms. Mendez, the science teacher, in the fall. Mr. Kylo noticed that Christi, one of the students with a learning disability with whom he had worked the previous year, was enrolled in Ms. Mendez's science class. Mr. Kylo knew that Christi had difficulty organizing information and studying. Recently, he had noticed that more and more students seemed to be struggling with the science curriculum as the district attempted to upgrade curriculum standards. Also, Ms. Mendez was experimenting with moving away from the book and creating her own organization for units and lessons. This would mean that neither he nor Christi's parents could rely on the textbook structure to help her learn the content and study.

Mr. Kylo met with Ms. Mendez over the summer and explained his concerns about Christi's success in her class. After being reassured that course content would not be watered down and that the adaptations could be used with the entire class, Mr. Kylo worked with Ms. Mendez to create organizers for the course. Together, they created a Course Organizer that would be used to launch the course, several Unit Organizers for the first semester of study, and a few Lesson Organizers for particularly difficult lessons. After Ms. Mendez started working with the organizers, she told Mr. Kylo that they really helped her to organize the information and to see why some of the content was difficult for students.

On the first day of school, Ms. Mendez and Mr. Kylo used the Course Organizer to introduce the course. Ms. Mendez presented and discussed the course questions and the course map with students, and Mr. Kylo led the class in completing the rest of the sections of the Course Organizer.

On parent night, they used the Course Organizer to preview the course for parents. Each parent received a copy of the Course Organizer. Christi's mother asked whether all the students in the class would be expected to answer all the questions. Ms. Mendez stated that every student would be able to talk about and provide accurate information related to each question by the end of the year.

In class, Ms. Mendez introduced the first unit using the unit organizer. She explained how the Unit Organizer would be used throughout the year and then introduced the first unit on energy. Each student created his or her own version of the organizer on a blank form. In the days that followed, Ms. Mendez kept returning to the Unit Organizer to bring the class back together. For students who had forgotten or lost their organizers, she put one on the bulletin board to copy. She noticed that Christi always had hers and that she was using it daily.

Mr. Kylo wondered whether Christi was using the Unit Organizer to review what she was learning. To check, he sat down with her one day and discovered that she could use the Unit Organizer as a guide to summarize and paraphrase what she was learning. In fact, he also found that she could describe the parts of the unit from memory and could use the self-test questions to elaborate on what she was learning.

Toward the end of the unit, Ms. Mendez introduced the first Lesson Organizer for a lesson that was particularly difficult. Since students were familiar with the Unit Organizer, they quickly learned how to fill in and use the Lesson Organizer form.

At the end of the unit, the class used their organizers to review for the test. Christi and another student paired up to test each other with the self-test questions and practice talking through the unit content map. Christi took the Unit and Lesson Organizers home and used them to review with her mother. Ms. Mendez allowed students to refer to the Unit Organizer as they took the test and gave students points for turning in the Unit Organizer when they completed the test.

On leaving the classroom after the test, Christi approached Ms. Mendez and asked her for a blank Unit Organizer. When Ms. Mendez asked Christi why she wanted it, Christi said that she wanted to use it in her American history class to organize the information.

Christi's grade on the unit test (a high C) was higher than any grade she had received the previous year (she had failed most of the tests). After the unit test, Ms. Mendez asked the class to get out their Course Organizers and directed their attention to the course questions and course map that she had placed on the bulletin board. The class reviewed which questions they could and could not answer, where they were in the course, how the course was going, and what needed to be changed. Ms. Mendez then began the next unit with a new Unit Organizer. Tests over subsequent units indicated that Christi was learning the information.

After several units, Ms. Mendez was unable to prepare a Unit Organizer before she introduced the unit. Several days into the unit, Christi and other students approached Ms. Mendez and asked her if she could help them construct Unit Organizers to help them study. Ms. Mendez told them she would restart the unit with a Unit Organizer that the whole class could use.

Who Can Provide Additional Information?

Coordinator of Training
Center for Research on Learning
University of Kansas
3061 Dole Center
Lawrence, KS 66045
785/864-4780
Website: www.ku-crl.org

What Other Information Is Available?

Bulgren, J. A., & Lenz, B. K. Strategic instruction in the content-areas. In D. Deshler, E. Ellis, & B. K. Lenz (Eds.), *Teaching the learning disabled adolescent: Strategies and methods*. Denver: Love.

Ellis, E. S., & Lenz, B. K. (1990). Techniques for mediating content-area learning: Issues and research. *Focus on Exceptional Children, 22*(9), 1–16.

Lenz, B. K. (1992). Self-managed learning strategy systems for children and youth. *School Psychology Review, 21*, 210–227.

Lenz, B. K., Bulgren, J. A., & Hudson, P. (1990). Content enhancement: A model for promoting the acquisition of content learning by individuals with learning disabilities. In T. Scruggs & B. Wong (Eds.), *Intervention research in learning disabilities* (pp. 122–165). Boston: Springer-Verlag.

Lenz, B. K., with Bulgren, J. A., Schumaker, J. B., Deshler, D. D., & Boudah, D. J. (1994). *The Unit Organizer Routine*. Lawrence, KS: Edge Enterprises.

Lenz, B. K., Deshler, D. D., & Schumaker, J. B. (1998). *The Course Organizer Routine*. Lawrence, KS: Edge Enterprises.

Lenz, B. K., Marrs, R., Schumaker, J. B., & Deshler, D. D. (1993). *The Lesson Organizer Routine*. Lawrence, KS: Edge Enterprises.

References

Lenz, B. K., Alley, G. R., & Schumaker, J. B. (1987). Activating the inactive learner: Advance organizers in the secondary content classroom. *Learning Disability Quarterly, 10*(1), 53–67.

Lenz, B. K., with Bulgren, J. A., Schumaker, J. B., Deshler, D. D., & Boudah, D. J. (1994). *The Unit Organizer Routine*. Lawrence, KS: Edge Enterprises.

Lenz, K., Deshler, D., Schumaker, J., Bulgren, J., Kissam, B., Vance, M., Roth, J., & McKnight, M. (1993). *The course planning routine: A guide for inclusive course planning.* (Research Report). Lawrence: Center for Research on Learning, University of Kansas.

5. Concept Organizers

Systems that emphasize the teaching of higher-order thinking skills (e.g., The National Commission on Excellence in Education, 1983; U.S. Department of Education, 1991) present a challenge to both teachers and students. In inclusive classrooms all students are expected to acquire and manipulate a variety of complex concepts and integrate these concepts with assumed prior knowledge. However, many students with disabilities have not mastered the strategies required to explore concepts independently and often do not have the same sets of background experiences and knowledge as their peers.

The three teaching routines that follow can help students acquire conceptual knowledge and critical thinking skills as part of group instruction. In these routines the teacher selects difficult but important concepts from the curriculum and adapts the presentation of each concept with diagrams known as *devices* that emphasize critical features of the concepts to make characteristics and relationships explicit. (Devices are instructional techniques designed to achieve a specific goal in promoting learning.) Then the teacher uses these devices to explore conceptual information through a teaching routine.

The Adaptations

You can use the three concept-teaching routines to (1) connect information about a new concept to prior knowledge about a familiar concept (the Concept Anchoring Routine) (Bulgren, Schumaker, & Deshler, 1994), (2) introduce conceptual information (the Concept Mastery Routine) (Bulgren, Deschler, & Shumaker, 1995), or (3) compare and contrast two or more concepts (the Concept Comparison Routine) (Bulgren, Lenz, Schumaker, & Deshler, 1995). Each adaptation is based on a one-page visual teaching device. Common symbols and graphics across the teaching devices reinforce common concept components such as characteristics and examples. Symbols within a diagram or table highlight complex and abstract information and relationships in conceptual information to enhance student understanding. (In this discussion, a *concept* is a word or phrase that represents a category or class into which events, ideas, or objects can be grouped. Examples of concepts include *vertebrate, democracy, poem,* and *fraction.*)

To use these adaptations, first select a critical concept or concepts from the curriculum. Next, prepare a draft of the visual teaching device

---

FIGURE 11

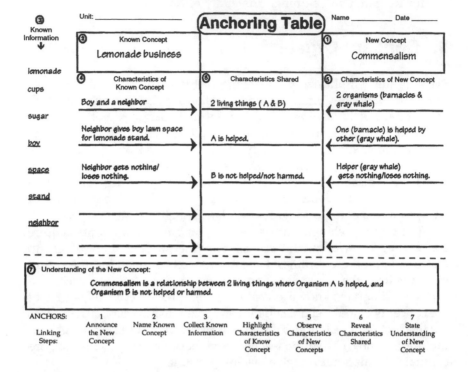

associated with a particular routine. Later, in class, distribute a blank version of the visual device to students. Then interactively build the final version of the visual teaching device with the students.

The Concept Anchoring Routine

The Concept Anchoring Routine (Bulgren et al., 1994) introduces new conceptual information to students and ties (or anchors) it to familiar information. This adaptation is based on a one-page visual teaching device called the *Concept Anchoring Table* (see Figure 11).

To create this table, use the background knowledge of students to develop an example, story, or analogy to anchor students' understanding of new conceptual information. When presenting the table to students, cue them that they will use the Anchoring Table to learn about a new, difficult, but important concept by building on knowledge they already have about a familiar concept.

Then create the table together with the class following these steps:

1. State the name of the new concept you have selected.

---

2. Announce the name of the known or familiar concept.

3. Pose questions that will help the students brainstorm what they know about the familiar concept. Have them write words (characteristics and examples) associated with the known conceptual information on the board and then on the table in an organized format.

4. Pose questions that will help the students see the similarities between each of the characteristics associated with the new concept.

5. Explore the shared characteristics—that is, the words or phrases that identify the larger groups that contain paired characteristics of both the known and the new concept.

6. Finally, ask students to create a summary of their understanding in a way that you specify; this may be a definition of the new conceptual information or an explanation of the analogy.

The Concept Mastery Routine

The Concept Mastery Routine (Bulgren et al., 1993) helps a class explore, review, or summarize a concept that has already been introduced. It is based on a one-page visual teaching device called the *Concept Diagram* (see Figure 12). To use the routine, cue students that they will use the Concept Diagram to summarize a difficult but important concept. Then review parts of the diagram if necessary, give rationales for learning the concept, and share your expectations about note-taking, participation, and understanding with them.

Next, do the diagram together. State the name of the concept and ask students to identify the overall concept. Then ask the students to brainstorm keywords (characteristics and examples) associated with the targeted concept. Together, sort key words into characteristics that are always, sometimes, and never present in the concept. Then, test possible examples from the keywords list by making sure that your examples have all of the characteristics that should always be present and none of the characteristics that can never be present in an example of a concept class. Propose new examples and together determine whether they are examples or nonexamples.

Finally, ask students to create a definition of the concept by organizing the name of the concept, the overall concept, and the characteristics that are always present into a coherent definition statement. The class can then revisit the Concept Diagram as needed and use it for further review and study.

FIGURE 12

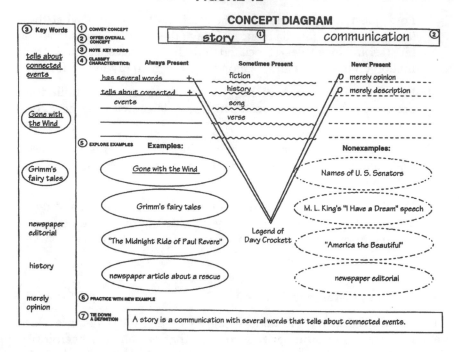

CONCEPT DIAGRAM

The Concept Comparison Routine

Once students begin to acquire information about important but difficult concepts, they face challenges related to encouraging higher-order thinking, which involves the manipulation of well-known concepts. The Concept Comparison Routine (Bulgren et al., 1995) helps a teacher lead students through such higher-order thinking processes. The Concept Comparison Routine is based on a one-page visual teaching device called the *Comparison Table* (see Figure 13).

To use the routine, cue students that the Comparison Table will help them explore related conceptual information, the importance of that information, and expectations regarding their participation. You will then create the table together.

State the names of two or more concepts (No. 1 in Figure 13) and ask students to identify the overall concept to which they are related (No. 2) and the characteristics of each concept (No. 3). Next, identify with them characteristics that the concepts have in common (No. 4), and then list some categories that describe those common characteristics (No. 5). Then proceed to identify characteristics of the targeted concepts that are not shared (No. 6), and for these, too, identify the larger categories into which these characteristics fit (No. 7). Finally, ask the

FIGURE 13

COMPARISON TABLE

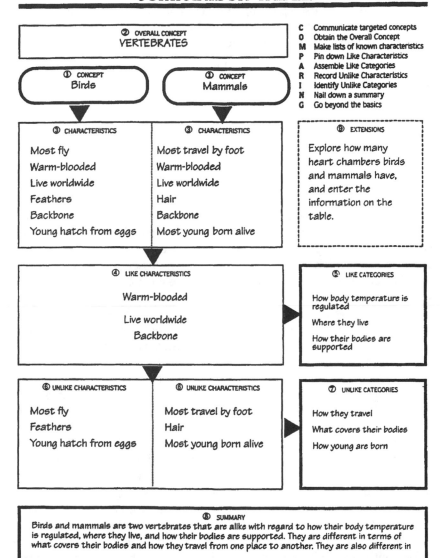

② OVERALL CONCEPT
VERTEBRATES

① CONCEPT
Birds

① CONCEPT
Mammals

C Communicate targeted concepts
O Obtain the Overall Concept
M Make lists of known characteristics
P Pin down Like Characteristics
A Assemble Like Categories
R Record Unlike Characteristics
I Identify Unlike Categories
N Nail down a summary
G Go beyond the basics

③ CHARACTERISTICS

Most fly
Warm-blooded
Live worldwide
Feathers
Backbone
Young hatch from eggs

③ CHARACTERISTICS

Most travel by foot
Warm-blooded
Live worldwide
Hair
Backbone
Most young born alive

⑨ EXTENSIONS

Explore how many heart chambers birds and mammals have, and enter the information on the table.

④ LIKE CHARACTERISTICS

Warm-blooded

Live worldwide

Backbone

⑤ LIKE CATEGORIES

How body temperature is regulated
Where they live
How their bodies are supported

⑥ UNLIKE CHARACTERISTICS

Most fly
Feathers
Young hatch from eggs

⑥ UNLIKE CHARACTERISTICS

Most travel by foot
Hair
Most young born alive

⑦ UNLIKE CATEGORIES

How they travel
What covers their bodies
How young are born

⑧ SUMMARY
Birds and mammals are two vertebrates that are alike with regard to how their body temperature is regulated, where they live, and how their bodies are supported. They are different in terms of what covers their bodies and how they travel from one place to another. They are also different in

students to summarize their understanding by explaining how the groups coincide or differ in terms of categories, characteristics, or both (No. 8). You may also ask the students to raise their own questions or to list insights gained from the comparison.

Across all three concept routines, you will use the following instructional sequence:

1. Cue the students regarding the use and benefits of the selected concept device and associated teaching routine, the importance of the information, and expectations for notetaking and participation.

2. Do the steps associated with the creation of the device collaboratively with the students.

3. Review the students' understanding of the conceptual information and the analysis you have used to guide the creation of each part of the device.

What Research Backs It Up?

Each of the teaching routines was validated in general education classes in which students with learning disabilities were enrolled. For example, research with 83 students in science classes has shown that students with learning disabilities and those who are low achieving, average achieving, and high achieving can all benefit when their teachers use the Concept Anchoring Routine (Bulgren, Deshler, & Schumaker, 1994). When students with learning disabilities were taught conceptual information with the use of the Concept Anchoring Routine, they earned scores that were, on average, 25% higher than on tests for which similar information was taught without Concept Anchoring (Bulgren, Deshler, Schumaker, & Lenz, 1999).

The Concept Mastery Routine produced similar improvements. It was empirically validated with a total of 475 students in 23 inclusive science and social studies secondary classes that included 32 students with learning disabilities. When their teachers used the Concept Mastery Routine rather than a traditional lecture-discussion format, students scored significantly better on tests designed to assess concept acquisition and on regular classroom tests. Groups of students with and without learning disabilities made comparable gains; on average, the scores of students with learning disabilities increased from 60% to 71% and those of students without learning disabilities from 72% to 87% on tests of concept acquisition. In addition, the percentage of students with and without learning disabilities who passed the tests increased. The students also took better notes, and both teachers and students were generally satisfied with the routine (Bulgren, 1987; Bulgren, Schumaker, & Deshler, 1988).

For the Concept Comparison Routine, research with 107 students enrolled in regular secondary science and social studies classes showed that low-achieving students, including students with learning disabilities, as well as average- and high-achieving students, correctly answered substantially more test questions related to information that had been presented through the use of the routine than test questions related to information presented using traditional teaching methods. Specifically, students with learning disabilities and other low-achieving students correctly answered an average of 71.2% and 86.4%, respectively, of the test questions associated with information presented through the use of the routine compared to 56.7% and 62.6% of the questions associated with information presented through traditional means (Bulgren, Schumaker, & Deshler, 1999).

What Does It Look Like in Practice?

Mark was a student with learning disabilities who struggled in his seventh-grade science class. He often felt lost during class discussions and rarely participated. Even though he had spent time in special education classrooms and had a repertoire of strategies to approach many individual learning situations, he did not have all of the prior knowledge needed to understand important and complex concepts such as vertebrates, mammals, reptiles, and amphibians.

His teacher, Mr. Lu, saw the need to incorporate specific instruction on conceptual information into his lessons to build on each student's background knowledge and to fill in background knowledge where needed. For example, he observed that students like Mark had heard the phrase "warm-blooded," but that they did not really understand many of the complexities associated with such concepts. Therefore, he decided to use a Concept Anchoring Table at the beginning of the unit on vertebrates to make certain that all students understood what the phrase "warm-blooded" meant, because it was critical conceptual information on which a great deal of later learning would be built.

Mr. Lu thought about the automatic temperature control function in vertebrates represented by the phrase "warm-blooded." He decided that the temperature control systems in modern buildings might serve as a perfect analogy to be used in the lesson. Temperature control systems in warm-blooded animals and temperature control systems in modern buildings both have a target temperature that is supposed to be maintained; they contain a mechanism that notices any temperature change; and this mechanism, when the internal temperature changes, sends signals that prompt other systems to correct the temperature. To make sure that the analogy would be appropriate, he asked Mark and some other students privately what they knew about temperature control systems in buildings such as their homes and the school. He determined that they knew enough to go forward with the analogy. He

FIGURE 14

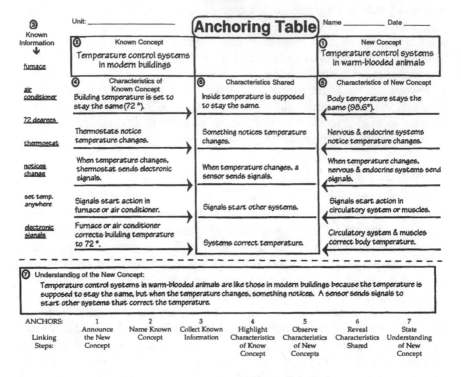

developed a Concept Anchoring Table to illustrate the analogy (see Figure 14).

Mr. Lu also wanted students to understand some concepts in depth. He assigned the students to read the chapter on vertebrates that dealt with mammals. To check that all of the students understood the concept of *mammals* thoroughly, he developed a Concept Diagram (Figure 15) in which he listed the key characteristics he wanted students to know about mammals. Then he developed four sets of examples and nonexamples and designed a progressively more difficult sequence to present these pairs. He began with the easy challenge of deciding whether humans and snakes were mammals and ended with the more difficult pairing of whales and sharks and bats and birds. He then selected an animal that could potentially be a mammal—the duckbilled platypus—and, as a homework assignment, he asked the students to apply the characteristics test to that choice and be prepared to argue the next day whether the duckbilled platypus was or was not a mammal.

Mr. Lu found the Concept Diagram particularly useful because he was able to introduce many terms related to higher-order thinking that

FIGURE 15

CONCEPT DIAGRAM

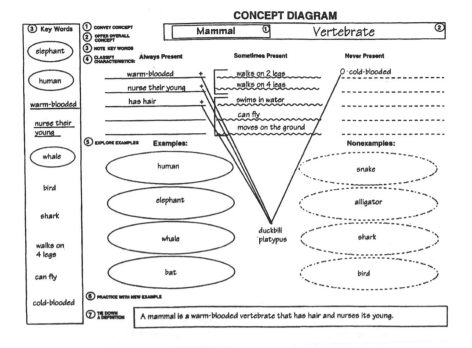

he would emphasize throughout the year. For example, he noticed that he would be able to cue students to:

- Start thinking about relationships between and among the overall concept, the targeted concept, and other concepts related to the targeted concept.

- Discriminate between examples and nonexamples.

- Analyze potential examples to see whether or not they have the pertinent characteristics that make them fit into the group.

- Synthesize characteristics into a definition of the concept.

Once the students seemed to understand the concept of a mammal, Mr. Lu proceeded to teach them about the four other vertebrate groups—fish, amphibians, reptiles, and birds. He thought that the students understood the differences, but as a final lesson he developed a Comparison Table to explore the similarities and differences among the five groups of vertebrates (see Figure 16).

He worked with the students so that they all indicated an understanding of the fact that fish, amphibians, reptiles, birds, and mammals

FIGURE 16
Multiple-Concept Comparison Table, p. 1

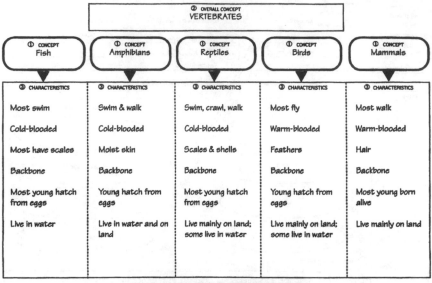

② OVERALL CONCEPT VERTEBRATES				
① CONCEPT Fish	① CONCEPT Amphibians	① CONCEPT Reptiles	① CONCEPT Birds	① CONCEPT Mammals
③ CHARACTERISTICS	③ CHARACTERISTICS	③ CHARACTERISTICS	③ CHARACTERISTICS	③ CHARACTERISTICS
Most swim	Swim & walk	Swim, crawl, walk	Most fly	Most walk
Cold-blooded	Cold-blooded	Cold-blooded	Warm-blooded	Warm-blooded
Most have scales	Moist skin	Scales & shells	Feathers	Hair
Backbone	Backbone	Backbone	Backbone	Backbone
Most young hatch from eggs	Young hatch from eggs	Most young hatch from eggs	Young hatch from eggs	Most young born alive
Live in water	Live in water and on land	Live mainly on land; some live in water	Live mainly on land; some live in water	Live mainly on land

STEPS 1-3 OF THE CONCEPT COMPARISON ROUTINE

Step 1: Communicate targeted concepts   Step 2: Obtain the Overall Concept   Step 3: Make lists of known characteristics

Multiple-Concept Comparison Table, p. 2

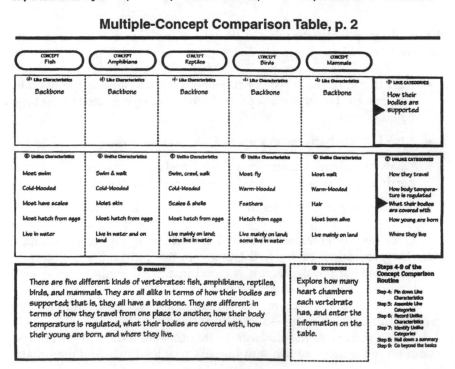

CONCEPT Fish	CONCEPT Amphibians	CONCEPT Reptiles	CONCEPT Birds	CONCEPT Mammals	
④ Like Characteristics	④ Like Characteristics	④ Like Characteristics	④ Like Characteristics	④ Like Characteristics	⑤ LIKE CATEGORIES
Backbone	Backbone	Backbone	Backbone	Backbone	▶ How their bodies are supported
⑥ Unlike Characteristics	⑥ Unlike Characteristics	⑥ Unlike Characteristics	⑥ Unlike Characteristics	⑥ Unlike Characteristics	⑦ UNLIKE CATEGORIES
Most swim	Swim & walk	Swim, crawl, walk	Most fly	Most walk	How they travel
Cold-blooded	Cold-blooded	Cold-blooded	Warm-blooded	Warm-blooded	How body temperature is regulated
Most have scales	Moist skin	Scales & shells	Feathers	Hair	▶ What their bodies are covered with
Most hatch from eggs	Most hatch from eggs	Most hatch from eggs	Hatch from eggs	Most born alive	How young are born
Live in water	Live in water and on land	Live mainly on land; some live in water	Live mainly on land; some live in water	Live mainly on land	Where they live

⑧ SUMMARY	⑨ EXTENSIONS	Steps 4-9 of the Concept Comparison Routine
There are five different kinds of vertebrates: fish, amphibians, reptiles, birds, and mammals. They are all alike in terms of how their bodies are supported; that is, they all have a backbone. They are different in terms of how they travel from one place to another, how their body temperature is regulated, what their bodies are covered with, how their young are born, and where they live.	Explore how many heart chambers each vertebrate has, and enter the information on the table.	Step 4: Pin down Like Characteristics Step 5: Assemble Like Categories Step 6: Record Unlike Characteristics Step 7: Identify Unlike Categories Step 8: Nail down a summary Step 9: Go beyond the basics

were similar in how their bodies were supported; that is, they had backbones. He also checked that they understood the categories of difference—that is, how body temperature is regulated, what their bodies are covered with, how the young are born, and where they live. He asked the students to summarize their understanding of the comparison by asking them to explore the different means of locomotion for each vertebrate and to enter that information on the Comparison Tables they had developed.

He continued to inform students about important thinking skills associated with the devices. Specifically, with the Comparison Table, students were able to apply thinking associated with analysis of characteristics, clustering of characteristics into groups that are alike and different, categorization of characteristics, exploration of new questions, and synthesis of understanding.

Additionally, Mr. Lu cued students to use the table and diagrams as study supports for short essays on the topics covered. He cued them that the name of the targeted concept generally should appear in the topic sentence, that each component on the device comprised details, and that the summary usually provided a good conclusion. Therefore, through the use of the devices, he was able to ensure their understanding, teach thinking skills, and prepare students for meaningful assessments.

For Mark, the incorporation of these routines into Mr. Lu's instruction meant that his grades, on average, increased from a middle-level D to a high C. In addition, Mark began to really understand the concepts that were presented and discussed in class and to participate in the class discussions. He began to take an active part in the learning community.

Who Can Provide Additional Information?

Coordinator of Training
Center for Research on Learning
University of Kansas
3061 Dole Center
Lawrence, KS 66045
785/864-4780
Website: www.ku-crl.org

What Additional Information Is Available?

Bulgren, J. A., Deshler, D. D., & Schumaker, J. B. (1993). *The Concept Mastery Routine*. Lawrence, KS: Edge Enterprises.

Bulgren, J. A., Lenz, B. K., Schumaker, J. B., & Deshler, D. D. (1995). *The Concept Comparison Routine*. Lawrence, KS: Edge Enterprises.

Bulgren, J. A., Schumaker, J. B., & Deshler, D. D. (1994). *The Concept Anchoring Routine.* Lawrence, KS: Edge Enterprises.

References

Bulgren, J. A. (1987). *The development and validation of instructional procedures to teach concepts in secondary mainstream classes which contain students with learning disabilities.* Unpublished doctoral dissertation, University of Kansas, Lawrence.

Bulgren, J. A., Deshler, D. D., Schumaker, J. B., & Lenz, B. K. (1999). *The use and effectiveness of a Concept Anchoring Routine in diverse secondary content classrooms.* Unpublished research report. Lawrence: Center for Research on Learning, University of Kansas.

Bulgren, J. A., & Lenz, B. K. (1996). Strategic instruction in the content-areas. In D. D. Deshler, E. S. Ellis, & B. K. Lenz (Eds.), *Teaching adolescents with learning disabilities: Strategies and methods* (2nd ed., pp. 409–473). Denver: Love.

Bulgren, J. A., Schumaker, J. B., & Deshler, D. D. (1988). Effectiveness of a concept teaching routine in enhancing the performance of LD students in secondary-level mainstream classes. *Learning Disabilities Quarterly, 11*(1), 3–17.

Bulgren, J. A., Schumaker, J. B., & Deshler, D. D. (1997a). *Effectiveness of a Concept Comparison Routine in enhancing the academic performance of secondary level students with and without learning disabilities.* Unpublished research report. Lawrence: Center for Research on Learning, University of Kansas.

Bulgren, J. A., Schumaker, J. B., & Deshler, D. D. (1997b). *Use of analogical anchoring by teachers in secondary level mainstream classes.* Lawrence: Center for Research on Learning, University of Kansas.

Lenz, B. K., & Bulgren, J. A. (1995). Promoting learning in the content-areas. In P. A. Cegelka & W. H. Berdine (Eds.), *Effective instruction for students with learning problems* (pp. 385–417). Needham Heights, MA: Allyn & Bacon.

Lenz, B. K., Bulgren, J. A., & Hudson, P. (1990). Content enhancement: A model for promoting the acquisition of content learning by individuals with learning disabilities. In T. Scruggs & B. Wong (Eds.), *Intervention in learning disabilities* (pp. 122–165). Boston: Springer-Verlag.

The National Commission on Excellence in Education. (1983). *A nation at risk: The imperative for educational reform.* Washington, DC: National Science Foundation.

U.S. Department of Education. (1991). *America 2000: An education strategy source book.* Washington, DC: U.S. Government Printing Office.

6. Mnemonic Adaptations

Textbooks in content-areas such as science, health, literature, foreign languages, and social studies are difficult to read for many students with disabilities, given that they often exceed the students' reading levels (Chiang-Soong & Yager, 1993). This difficulty is compounded because the texts also contain numerous unfamiliar vocabulary words; names of famous individuals, places, and things; concepts; and associated information. The sheer amount of new, unfamiliar information presented to students with disabilities can be overwhelming in itself, but their problems increase when all of the unfamiliar information is presented in formats written above their grade levels. Unfortunately, students' grades in content-area classes are based predominantly on their performance on tests covering information in their textbooks (Putnam, 1992b), and teacher-made exams emphasize recollection of factual information (Putnam, 1992a). Not surprisingly, students with disabilities, many of whom have memory difficulties, often perform poorly on such tests (Cooney & Swanson, 1987).

This adaptation was developed to facilitate the learning and recollection of unfamiliar vocabulary and definitions, names of people or places and what they are famous for, and other factual information across all content-areas.

The Adaptation

To use this adaptation, develop specific mnemonic devices for each unfamiliar word, person, place, or thing and the associated information that is to be remembered. The mnemonic devices make unfamiliar words more familiar, integrate the words with the related information, and strengthen students' encoding and retrieval skills. This, in turn, promotes initial learning and delayed recall of the information. The specific steps involved in developing the mnemonic devices and helping students learn them are as follows:

Step 1: Identify the unfamiliar word, person, place, or thing and the associated information.

Step 2: Change the unfamiliar word into one that is familiar but is acoustically similar and easily pictured, called a *keyword*.

Step 3: Make an interactive picture of the recorded word (keyword) and the related information.

FIGURE 17
Mnemonic Representation of George M. Cohan

Note. Reprinted with permission from Mastropieri, M. A., & Scruggs, T. E. (1991). *Teaching students ways to remember: Strategies for learning mnemonically.* Cambridge, MA: Brookline Books.

Step 4: Present the keyword and picture in class and set up practice opportunities for students to use the devices to retrieve information.

For example, you might first decide that students need to remember that George M. Cohan is a famous songwriter who composed the World War I song "Over There" (Mastropieri & Scruggs, 1991). If the name *Cohan* is unfamiliar, recode it into the acoustically similar word *cone* (as in "ice cream cone"), which is easily pictured. Next, make an interactive picture of the newly created keyword *(cone)* and the information related to the songwriter who composed "Over There." You might create a picture of a child with an ice cream cone, people asking the child "Where did you get that cone?", and the child responding by singing the song "Over There." (See Figure 17.)

Then you can present the information in class and explain to the students that when they are asked to remember the information associated with George M. Cohan, they can think of the keyword *cone* because it sounds like the name *Cohan*. Students will thus have a direct retrieval route to the song "Over There" because of the interactive picture that came between the keyword and the associated information. Finally, you can have the students practice asking themselves or each

FIGURE 18
Mnemonic Representation for the Number of Legs on an Insect

Note. Reprinted with permission from Mastropieri, M. A., & Scruggs, T. E. (1993). *A practical guide for teaching science to students with special needs in inclusive settings.* Austin, TX: Pro-Ed.

other the question "Why was George Cohen famous?", thinking of the keyword and picture, and answering the question until they feel comfortable retrieving the information.

This keyword method can be applied successfully to learning new and unfamiliar information across all content-areas. Sometimes, however, students are required to learn numbered or ordered information, such as hardness levels of minerals or the sequence of U.S. presidents. In these cases, a pegword can be substituted for the keyword in the steps listed above. *Pegwords* are rhyming words for numbers, such as the following: one is *bun,* two is *shoe,* three is *tree,* four is *door,* five is *hive,* six is *sticks,* seven is *heaven,* eight is *gate,* nine is *vine,* ten is *hen.*

For example, you might decide that students need to remember that insects have six legs. Since the number six is included in the information, think of the pegword for six, which is *sticks.* Then make an interactive picture of the pegword and the associated information, such as insects with six legs walking along sticks (for *six*) (see Figure 18).

Next, you present the pegword and picture to students and explain that when they are asked how many legs insects have, they are to recall the interactive picture containing the insects, remember that the insects were walking along sticks, which is the pegword for *six,* and retrieve

FIGURE 19
Mnemonic Representation of
"The State Capital of Louisiana Is Baton Rouge"

Louisiana   Baton Rouge
(Louise, Anna)   (baton, rouge)

Note. Reprinted with permission from Mastropieri, M. A., & Scruggs, T. E. (1992). Copyrighted materials.

the information that insects have six legs. Finally, you would program sufficient practice opportunities for students to learn the steps involved in recalling the information.

Keywords and pegwords can be combined in various ways to meet the learning demands associated with complex sets of information. When two pieces of information that are associated are both unfamiliar, two keywords can be used, as may be necessary in learning the names of the states and their capitals. For example, to learn that the capital of Louisiana is Baton Rouge, keywords need to be developed for both Louisiana and Baton Rouge. Good keywords for Louisiana could be *Louise* and *Anna,* and for Baton Rouge *baton* and *rouge.* An interactive picture containing all of these keywords might include two girls, Louise and Anna, who are wearing rouge and twirling batons (see Figure 19).

Keywords and pegwords can be combined in the same picture. For example, to help students learn that the mineral wolframite is a four on the Mohs hardness scale, you could create a keyword for wolframite, which in this case could be *wolf.* Next, you would recall the pegword

Note. Reprinted with permission from Scruggs, T. E., Mastropieri, M. A., Levin, J. R., & Gaffney, J. S. (1985). Facilitating the acquisition of science facts in learning disabled students. *Amerian Educational Research Journal, 22,* 575–586.

for four, which is *floor.* Then you would generate an interactive picture of the keyword *wolf* and the pegword *floor* doing something together, such as a wolf standing on the floor (Figure 20). You would explain to your students that when they are asked to retrieve the information, they can do it in one of two ways. On the one hand, when asked what the hardness level of wolframite is, they should remember the keyword *wolf* and then the interactive image of the wolf standing on the floor. Then they should remember that the pegword *floor* represents *four.* When they are asked what mineral is four on the hardness scale, they should remember the pegword for four, which is *floor,* and the interactive picture with the floor in it. Next, they should recall the rest of the picture, which contains the keyword *wolf,* and this will lead to *wolframite.* Once this has been explained, you can set up opportunities for students to practice retrieving information both ways.

What Research Backs It Up?

Numerous research studies support the efficacy of the mnemonic keyword method with students who have disabilities (Mastropieri & Scruggs, in press; Scruggs & Mastropieri, 1990). Initial investigations focused on instruction of students with mild disabilities in one-to-one learning situations, while later studies involved extended classroom-based instruction delivered by teachers (Mastropieri & Scruggs, 1989a; Scruggs & Mastropieri, 1990). Mnemonic adaptations have been validated across many grades and age levels—for example, fourth-grade students with mild disabilities in Indiana history (Mastropieri & Scruggs, 1989b); fourth- and fifth-grade students with disabilities in English vocabulary (Berry, 1986; Condus, Marshall, & Miller, 1986) and science (Scruggs, Mastropieri, Levin, & Gaffney, 1985; Scruggs, Mastropieri, Levin, McLoone, et al., 1985); and junior and senior high school students in science and social studies (Mastropieri, Scruggs, & Whedon, 1997; Mastropieri, Scruggs, Whittaker, & Bakken, 1994) and vocabulary (Mastropieri & Scruggs, in press).

In all studies, when students with mild disabilities were taught using mnemonic strategies, they consistently outperformed their control counterparts on immediate and delayed recall measures. All students also reported enjoying instruction more when it included mnemonic strategies. Although students with mild disabilities have also been taught successfully to create their own mnemonic strategies (Fulk, Mastropieri, & Scruggs, 1992), their performance is frequently lower than it is when teachers prepare and present the strategies. The amount of time students require to cover the same amount of content is also longer because they require extensive time to develop their own strategies (Scruggs & Mastropieri, 1992).

What Does It Look Like in Practice?

Mr. Roth, a science teacher, decided that his students needed to learn the hardness of wolframite and that it is black and is used in making light bulbs. He created a picture of a black wolf standing on a floor that is lit by light bulbs (see Figure 20). He introduced the information to his students in the following way:

Mr. Roth: Let's think of a good way to help you remember that wolframite is four on the hardness scale, black in color, and used in making light bulbs. Remember how we used keywords and pegwords before? A good keyword for wolframite is *wolf,* because it sounds like *wolframite* and is easily pictured. What is the keyword for wolframite?

Students: Wolf.

Mr. Roth: Remember that pegwords are rhyming words for numbers. What is a good pegword for *four?*

Students: Floor.

Mr. Roth: Right! *Floor* is a good pegword because it rhymes with *four.* Now let's make a good interactive picture with a wolf and floor. How about a wolf standing on a checkered floor? See our picture? The wolf and the floor are doing something together. Now let's add in the other pieces of information that we need to remember with wolframite. Wolframite is black in color, so let's imagine that the wolf in our picture is black. That will help us remember that wolframite is black in color. Now we also need to remember that wolframite is used for making light bulbs. Let's have the floor being lit up by a row of light bulbs. Now we have every piece of information we need to remember this picture. What is happening in the picture, class?

Students: A black wolf is standing on the floor that is lit up by light bulbs.

Mr. Roth: Good. Now tell me what all of that represents.

Students: Wolf is for wolframite, black is for black color, floor is four—four on the hardness scale—and light bulbs are how wolframite is used.

Mr. Roth: Great, let's practice that again so we remember the important information about wolframite. What if I were to ask you to tell me all you know about wolframite? What would you think of first?

Mr. Roth continued to prompt the students through the retrieval of the keyword and pegword and picture until he was certain the students had learned the information. Then, on subsequent days, during a quick review at the beginning of class, he asked the students to recall the devices associated with wolframite and other key concepts. On the day of the test, he prompted the students to use the mnemonic devices to help them answer the questions on the test. As a result, students who might have received failing grades on the test had they not learned the devices received passing grades.

Who Can Provide Additional Information?

Professors Margo A. Mastropieri and Thomas E. Scruggs
Graduate School of Education
George Mason University
MSN 4B3
4400 University Drive
Fairfax, VA 22030-4444
703/993-4136
E-mail: mmastrop@gmu.edu

What Additional Information Is Available?

Mastropieri, M. A., & Scruggs, T. E. (1991). *Teaching students ways to remember: Strategies for learning mnemonically.* Cambridge, MA: Brookline.

References

Berry, J. K. (1987). *Learning-disabled children's use of mnemonic strategies for vocabulary learning.* Unpublished doctoral dissertation, University of Wisconsin, Madison.

Chiang-Soong, B., & Yager, R. E. (1993). Readability levels of the science textbooks most used in secondary schools. *School Science and Mathematics, 93*(1), 24–27.

Condus, M. M., Marshall, K. J., & Miller, S. R. (1986). Effects of the keyword mnemonic strategy on vocabulary acquisition and maintenance by learning disabled children. *Journal of Learning Disabilities, 19,* 609–613.

Cooney, J. B., & Swanson, H. L. (1987). Memory and learning disabilities: An overview. In H. L. Swanson (Ed.), *Advances in learning and behavioral disabilities, supplement 2: Memory and learning disabilities* (pp. 1–40). Greenwich, CT: JAI.

Fulk, B. J. M., Mastropieri, M. A., & Scruggs, T. E. (1992). Mnemonic generalization training with learning disabled adolescents. *Learning Disabilities Research and Practice, 7,* 2–10.

Mastropieri, M. A., & Scruggs, T. E. (1989a). Constructing more meaningful relationships: Mnemonic instruction for special populations. *Educational Psychology Review, 1,* 83–111.

Mastropieri, M. A., & Scruggs, T. E. (1989b). Mnemonic social studies instruction: Classroom applications. *Remedial and Special Education, 20*(3), 40–46.

Mastropieri, M. A., & Scruggs, T. E. (in press). Constructing more meaningful relationships in the classroom: Mnemonic research into practice. *Learning Disabilities Research & Practice.*

Mastropieri, M. A., Scruggs, T. E., & Whedon, C. (1997). Using mnemonic strategies to teach information about U.S. presidents: A classroom-based investigation. *Learning Disability Quarterly, 20,* 13–21.

Mastropieri, M. A., Scruggs, T. E., Whittaker, M. E. S., & Bakken, J. P. (1994). Applications of mnemonic strategies with students with mental disabilities. *Remedial and Special Education, 15* (1), 34–43.

Putnam, M. L. (1992a). Characteristics of questions on tests administered by mainstream secondary classroom teachers. *Learning Disabilities Research & Practice, 7,* 129–136.

Putnam, M. L. (1992b). The testing practices of mainstream secondary classroom teachers. *Remedial and Special Education, 13*(5), 11–21.

Scruggs, T. E., & Mastropieri, M. A. (1990). The case for mnemonic instruction: From laboratory investigations to classroom applications. *Journal of Special Education, 24,* 7–29.

Scruggs, T. E., & Mastropieri, M. A. (1992). Classroom applications of mnemonic instruction: Acquisition, maintenance, and generalization. *Exceptional Children, 58,* 219–229.

Scruggs, T. E., Mastropieri, M. A., Levin, J. R., & Gaffney, J. S. (1985). Facilitating the acquisition of science facts in learning disabled students. *American Educational Research Journal, 22,* 575–586.

Scruggs, T. E., Mastropieri, M. A., Levin, J. R., McLoone, B. B., Gaffney, J. S., & Prater, M. (1985). Increasing content-area learning: A comparison of mnemonic and visual-spatial direct instructions. *Learning Disabilities Research, 1,* 18–31.

7. Problem-Solving Prompts for Performance Assessments

Since the 1997 reauthorization of the Individuals with Disabilities Education Act (IDEA), students with disabilities are required to take part in all large-scale assessments at the district and/or state level. In 1994, 45 states conducted large-scale assessments in math, language arts, writing, science, and social science (Bond, Breskamp, & Roeber, 1996). The remaining states are expected to follow suit. In most of these testing programs, a standards model has been applied in which students must demonstrate a high level of proficiency. Furthermore, these testing programs rely on reading and writing skills to assess content-areas such as math, social studies, and science. In these tests, students are required to think critically and solve problems. Often these performance tasks surprise students, introduce unfamiliar terms, and do not clearly specify the required response.

Unfortunately, many students with learning disabilities have poor language skills, exhibit difficulty following directions, have poor test-taking skills, and show limited understanding of abstract ideas (Atwood & Oldham, 1985; Casby, 1989; Mastropieri & Scruggs, 1995). This adaptation was designed to help these students participate more fully in performance assessments and demonstrate their knowledge and skills in the topic area more effectively.

The Adaptation

The adaptation involves teacher creation of a series of prompts associated with each performance assessment task. Through the use of these prompts, the format and informational content of the original question are altered and expanded upon. The prompts (a) provide an introduction and context for the problem, (b) make students aware of the concepts to be understood within the content, and (c) cue the students as to what "thinking" responses to use when solving the problem. These new prompts clearly align the problem to be solved with the content and instruction and provide students with familiar key terms. They format the performance assessment in a way that does not surprise students or force them to make multiple inferences. These new prompts typically result in more text than the original, but the information is better organized for students, and the prompts can be read aloud.

What Research Backs It Up?

This adaptation has been used in a series of studies in the content-areas in which subject-matter content in middle schools has been modified to provide students better access to discipline knowledge (Hollenbeck & Tindal, 1996; Nolet & Tindal, 1994, 1995; Tindal & Nolet, 1996; Tindal, Rebar, Nolet, & McCollum, 1995). The most recent study used a multiple-baseline across-students design within a 7-week unit on geography. A series of problem-solving performance assessments were used to measure the geographic knowledge of six middle-school students. The assessments were adapted from questions provided in the text and were administered biweekly in a general education social studies classroom.

The students were taught to analyze the assessment prompts, identify the key concepts and response mode, and organize information through a comprehensive instructional intervention that included explicit teaching, modeling, and feedback. Prior to this prompt adaptation and instructional intervention, assessment outcomes for five students demonstrated no positive slope, with scores ranging from 0 to 2 on a 6-point scale. During the instructional phase, scores ranged from 1 to 6, reflecting positive slopes for five students that clearly corresponded to the adaptation and intervention. Although one participant showed a nonlinear slope during the intervention phase, all student scores increased and reflected responses demonstrating greater geographic knowledge.

What Does It Look Like in Practice?

Mr. George, a middle-school teacher, wanted to test his students' understanding throughout a social studies unit that was centered on the following standard: "Understand how the characteristics of different physical environments provide opportunities for or place constraints on human activities" (Geography Standards Education Project, 1994, p. 173). To explicate this standard and provide students with a foundation from which to engage in and manipulate information, Mr. George framed his instruction and assessments with concepts (Tindal, Nolet, & Blake, 1992). The concepts and attributes (noted in parentheses) were as follows:

- Regions (cultural, geographic, economic, political).

- Culture (language, beliefs, ethnicity, socioeconomic status, age).

- Economic systems (exchange, natural resources, labor, manufacturing).

- Political systems (laws, public service, decision making, systems of influence).

- Geography (landforms, area, map, climate).

In addition, throughout instruction, students were required to manipulate these concepts in a number of ways to show thinking in their responses: reiteration, summarization, illustration, prediction, evaluation, and explanation (Williams & Haladyna, 1982).

When Mr. George reviewed the test prompts in the text, he found the following sample problem among other problems that were similar: "Why do more people live in the western section of California than in the eastern section?" Mr. George decided that this prompt was ill defined and would not provide students who had disabilities the focus and structure to accommodate their language skill deficits or engage their thinking around the unit concepts. To carefully adapt this task, Mr. George used a prompt construction guide (Figure 21) to plan the adaptation. Once the adaptation was planned, Mr. George then placed the prompts within a standard performance assessment format (Figure 22).

Step 1: Introductory Prompt

Mr. George first used the introduction to establish the broad area of the content, the setting for the problem, and the context of the task. The unit content and instruction were framed around concepts that highlighted the relationship between geographic and human systems. Therefore, Mr. George aligned the introductory section of the prompt to his instruction by defining the broad area of the content (i.e., geography and human systems), the setting (i.e., California, mid-1800s), and the context (i.e., decisions about migration of individuals and settlement).

FIGURE 21

Original Prompt	Prompt Guidelines	Adapted Prompt
"Why do more people live in the western section of California than in the eastern section?"	*Step 1. Introductory Prompt* Establish the broad area of the content (topic), the setting for the problem, and the context of the task.	"Below is a map of California showing the landforms of the region and the major cities. Look at the map, and pretend it is the mid-1800s. You are leading a small group of families on a wagon train to live in California.
	Step 2. Concepts Prompt Focus attention on concepts.	"You have been in California many times and have learned much about the state and its geography and economic, political, and cultural systems. The people you are bringing ask you to recommend a good place for them to settle.
	Step 3. Prompt Responses The response demands made upon students should ensure that they are performing the correct intellectual operations to create their answers.	"First, place a large X on the map showing the location where you think these families should settle. "Now, explain why the location you picked would be a good place for these families to settle. Remember to use specific ideas about geography and economic, political, and cultural systems when writing your answer. "Before you start to write, list the important concepts and attributes at the bottom of this page and then use them in phrases."

FIGURE 22
Adapted Problem-Solving Assessment

RELOCATION

"Below is a map of California showing the landforms of the region and the major cities. Look at the map and pretend it is the mid-1800s. You are leading a small group of families on a wagon train to live in California. You have been in California many times and have learned much about the state and its geography and economic, political, and cultural systems. The people you are bringing ask you to recommend a good place for them to settle. Think about what you know about geography and its influence on economic, political, and cultural systems to choose a place that would be good for these families to live."

RELOCATION

"First, place a large X on the map showing the location where you think these families should settle.

"Now, explain why the location you picked would be a good place for these families to settle. Remember to use specific ideas about geography and economic, political, and cultural systems when writing your answer.

"Before you begin to write your answer, list the concepts and attributes at the bottom of this page, and then use them in phrases."

_____

_____

_____

_____

_____

_____

_____

_____

_____

_____

Step 2: Concepts Prompt

The second part of the adaptation provided a range of instructional concepts not included in the original prompt that could be used within the specific context and content established in the introductory prompt. To help facilitate their thinking and manipulation of information, Mr. George created a prompt to focus students on considering the relationship between geography and human systems. He embedded within the prompt the exact concepts to be taught: economical, political, and cultural systems.

Step 3: Prompt Responses

The third step required an explicit specification of the responses needed to solve the problem. In the original prompt, students were directed to answer "why." This directive did not delineate the exact response desired and had the potential outcome of students responding in different ways. Mr. George therefore included two response directives. Part 1 ("First . . .") was intended to prompt students to build and organize their response. Part 2 ("Now, explain . . .") prompted them to complete their response with a particular intellectual operation that had been practiced throughout instruction.

Mr. George also taught the students a strategy to help them structure their written responses. First they were taught to identify the concepts they would use in their answer and write them at the bottom of their paper. Then they were taught to list the attributes next to each concept. Finally, they were taught to organize those lines of information into phrases and to use those phrases as the foundation of their written answers. Mr. George instructed them to write these responses immediately below the prompt in the first half of the paper. This strategy was designed to (a) warm students up before they began writing and (b) focus them on a response immediately following the prompt that was focused and connected.

Students in Mr. George's class were prepared for and benefited from this adapted performance assessment in the knowledge and the response needed to solve the problem, even though it was novel for them. It was clearly aligned with the content and instruction of the class and was formatted in a manner that would not surprise them or force them to make multiple inferences. The prompt was aligned with instruction and served as a natural extension of instruction, providing them with familiar key terms (both concepts and "thinking" responses.) During instruction and practice tasks, students were taught to (a) look for key concepts within the prompts and on the accompanying maps and (b) list them at the bottom of their papers to help them write their answers above. Finally, although the adapted prompt contained far more text, the information was more organized, and it was read aloud to students.

Students should not be given a performance task that surprises them, introduces unfamiliar terms, or does not clearly specify a response. For students to succeed on performance assessments, they need to be administered tasks that contain clear context, concepts, and responses. If these components are ill defined or are not aligned to instructional content or strategies, it is difficult to determine whether student performance is a result of poor knowledge and skills or problems in accessing the problem solution.

Who Can Provide Additional Information?

Jerry Tindal
Behavioral Research and Teaching
College of Education
5262 University of Oregon
Eugene, OR 97403-5262

References

Atwood, R. K., & Oldham, B. R. (1985). Teacher's perceptions of mainstreaming in an inquiry oriented elementary science program. *Science Education, 69*, 619–624.

Bond, L. A., Breskamp, D., & Roeber, E. (1996). The status report of the assessment programs in the United States: State Students Assessment Programs Database School Year 1994–1995. Oak Brook, IL: North Central Regional Educational Laboratory.

Casby, M. W. (1989). National data concerning communication disorders and special education. *Language, Speech, and Hearing Services in the Schools, 20*, 22–30.

Geography Standards Education Project. (1994). *Geography for life*. Washington, DC: National Georgraphic Society.

Hollenbeck, K., & Tindal, G. (1996). Teaching law concepts within mainstreamed middle school social studies settings. *Diagnostique, 21*(4), 37–58.

Mastropieri, M. A., & Scruggs, T. E. (1995). Teaching science to students with disabilities in general education settings. *TEACHING Exceptional Children, 27*(4), 10–13.

Nolet, V., & Tindal, G. (1994). Instruction and learning in middle school science classes: Implications for students with disabilities. *The Journal of Special Education, 28*, 166–187.

Nolet, V., & Tindal, G. (1995). Essays as valid measures of learning in middle school science classes. *Learning Disabilities Quarterly, 18*, 311–324.

Tindal, G., & Nolet, V. (1996). Serving students in middle school content classes: A heuristic study of critical variables linking instruction and assessment. *The Journal of Special Education, 29*, 414–432.

Tindal, G., Nolet, V. W., & Blake, G. (1992). Focus on teaching and learning in content classes. (Training Module No. 3). Eugene: Research, Consultation, and Training Program, University of Oregon.

Tindal, G., Rebar, M., Nolet, V., & McCollum, S. (1995). Understanding instructional outcome options for students with special needs in content classes. *Learning Disabilities: Research and Practice*, 10(2), 72–84

Williams, R. G., & Haladyna, T. M. (1982). Logical operations for generating intended questions (LOGIQ): A typology for higher order-level test items. In G. H. Roid & T. M. Haladyna (Eds.), *A technology for test-item writing* (pp. 161–186). New York: Academic.

8. The Survey Routine

Subject-area textbooks and other written materials are important resources in the middle grades. Students are expected to read and study these materials, and they are often asked to complete assignments associated with written materials by, for example, answering questions at the back of each chapter or completing worksheets about the information. These demanding tasks are often very difficult, if not impossible, for students with reading difficulties. Students with learning disabilities, on average, enter the middle grades reading at a level that is 3 years behind grade level. For example, seventh-graders with disabilities read, on average, at the fourth-grade level (Warner, Schumaker, Alley, & Deshler, 1980). Thus, it is very difficult for them to obtain information from their textbooks, which are written at the seventh-grade level or above. Inconsiderate textbook features (Armbruster, 1984) add yet another layer of difficulty. For example, textbooks are often poorly organized and confusing.

This adaptation is useful across content areas (e.g., English, science, social studies) to help teachers (a) analyze the features of their textbooks and other reading materials, (b) prepare students for their reading experiences and assignments associated with their textbooks, and (c) help the students create study guides for the information in their textbooks.

The Adaptation

This adaptation has three parts. In the first part, you analyze the textbook or other reading material to determine which features are inconsiderate for readers. Use a checklist of features (Deshler, Schumaker, & McKnight, 1997; Appendix, Figure A1) to review and evaluate various aspects of the reading material. Once the checklist is complete, you can determine actions that can make the material more accessible or learner friendly.

Next, prior to presenting each reading assignment to students, you should plan how to help the students survey the written material to identify the key information and how that information will be displayed visually. Figure 23 presents a draft of this graphic device, called the *TRIMS Learning Sheet*.

Finally, introduce the reading assignment to the students in class, and, through an interactive process called the *Survey Routine*, you can help the students create their own TRIMS Learning Sheets. Together, you and your students survey and discuss the title of the reading passage, its relationship to other passages in the same book, the introduction to the passage, its main sections, and the summary. As the discussion progresses, the students write key information on their TRIMS Learning Sheets, which become personal study guides for reading activities and information in the passage.

What Research Backs It Up?

To validate the Survey Routine, a research study was conducted in general education science and social studies classes in middle schools (Deshler, Schumaker, & McKnight, 1999) using a multiple-baseline across-classes design. The dependent measure was student performance on chapter tests prepared by the publisher of the textbook each teacher was using. Results of the study showed that students with disabilities as well as students with no disabilities scored on average about 12 percentage points higher on chapter tests when their teachers used the Survey Routine to introduce the chapter than when the teachers did not use the routine.

What Does It Look Like in Practice?

Mr. Willis noticed that whenever he asked his students to read in their seventh-grade science textbooks to prepare for an upcoming lesson, many of them were not completing their reading assignments. When he analyzed the textbook, he noticed that it was written at the eighth-grade level. He checked several of his students' files and realized that most were reading below that level, and some of them (like William, who was reading at the fourth-grade level) were reading far below that level. He also noticed, while using the Considerate Text Features Checklist (Deshler et al., 1997; Appendix, Figure A1), that several aspects of the textbook were inconsiderate. For example, the title and subheadings in the text were often misleading and not connected to the information. Key terms and other important information were not cued through the use of boldface print or italics.

Mr. Willis wanted to help his students learn how to get key information from their textbooks. Thus, he began using the Survey Routine. Before he was about to begin a new unit of instruction, he surveyed the next textbook chapter and created a draft of the TRIMS Learning Sheet.

FIGURE 23

Student Name: _Bob Nelson_

TRIMS Learning Sheet

Title

1. Title: _Senses and Behavior_

2. This is about _How our senses relate to our behavior_

Relationships

3.

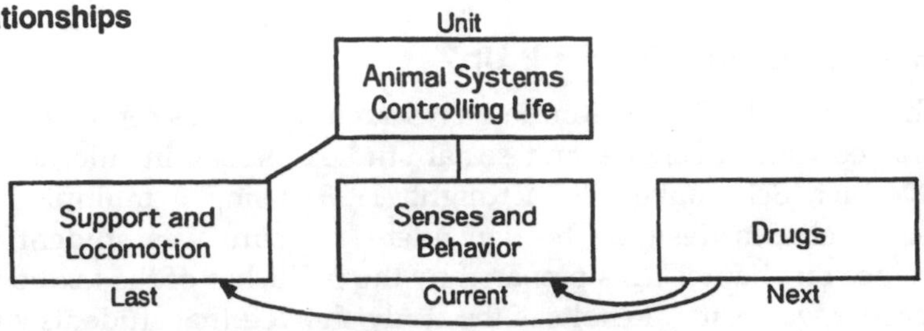

Unit

```
              ┌─────────────────────┐
              │   Animal Systems    │
              │   Controlling Life  │
              └─────────────────────┘
┌──────────────┐   ┌──────────────┐   ┌──────────────┐
│ Support and  │   │  Senses and  │   │              │
│  Locomotion  │   │   Behavior   │   │    Drugs     │
└──────────────┘   └──────────────┘   └──────────────┘
    Last              Current              Next
```

4. The relationship of current passage to the unit: _____
    The senses are one type of animal system that controls life.

5. The relationship of passages within the unit: _____
    Like the senses, support and locomotion are animal systems.
    Drugs affect our senses and how we move.

Introduction

6. • _Senses affect behavior from birth._
   • _Behavior is how a person acts._
   • _Sense organs - parts of the body that tell what is going on around us._

Main Parts

7. (Fill in next page)

Summary/Critical

8. • _Sense organs tell us what's happening around us._   _Sense organs have a special way of_
   taking in information.   _Each is made of parts that work together to give us information._
   • _What is common across the sense organs?   What is different?_

University of Kansas Center for Research on Learning January, 1997

Main Part #1: _The Eye_ _____ (pg. 274)

Questions

- _What are the parts of the eye and their jobs? (LINCS)_
- _What are the four steps of the light pathway? (LISTS)_
- _____

Parts & Job			Diagrams
Outside parts:	_Inside parts:_	_Lens Muscle_	_p. 274_
Eyelid _Iris_	_Cornea_	_Retina_	_p. 275 top_
Sclera _Pupil_	_Lens_	_Optic Nerve_	_p. 275 side_

Main Part #2: _The Tongue and Nose_ _____ (pg. 276)

Questions

- _What are the four types of tastes detected by tongue neurons? (LISTS)_
- _What are the seven types of smells detected by nose neurons? (LISTS)_
- _Why are the tongue and nose grouped together?_

Neuron Types		Diagrams
Tongue Neurons:	_Nose Neurons:_	_p. 276_
Bitter _Salty_		
Sour _Sweet_		

Main Part #3: _The Ear_ _____ (pg. 277)

Questions

- _What are the parts of the ear and their jobs? (LINCS)_
- _What are the steps of the sound pathway? (LISTS)_
- _What are sound waves? (LINCS)_

Parts & Job		Diagrams
Outer Ear _Ear Bones_		_p. 278 top_
Ear Canal _Oval Window_		_p. 278 bottom_
Ear Drum _Spiral Tube_		

University of Kansas Center for Research on Learning January, 1997

continues

FIGURE 23 *(Continued)*

Main Part #4:   *The Skin*   (pg. 279)

> **Questions**

- What are the kinds of changes skin neurons detect? (LISTS)
-
-

Neuron Types		Diagrams
Pain	Cold	p. 279
Pressure	Touch	
Heat		

Main Part #_ : _____

_____

- _____
- _____
- _____

Main Part #_ : _____

_____

- _____
- _____
- _____

University of Kansas Center for Research on Learning January, 1997

78

Then, in class, he put a blank form of the TRIMS Learning Sheet on the overhead projector and gave all his students their own blank versions of it. Next, he engaged them in a 15- to 20-minute discussion about this next chapter, focusing on the title, the relationship of the chapter to other chapters, the introduction, the main parts, and the summary.

As he asked the students questions, he was careful to involve students like William in the discussion. He was also careful to draw their attention to key terms and any features of the chapter that needed extra explanation. As he filled in each of the sections on the Learning Sheet, he circulated among the students to check that they were filling theirs in accurately. He then explained how his students could use the Learning Sheets as they read and studied the chapter.

Over time, Mr. Willis began giving his students more and more responsibility for filling out the Learning Sheets on their own. After guiding them through the process several times, he had them complete the Learning Sheets in cooperative groups and then in pairs. Finally, he began assigning the Learning Sheets as homework. As a result, Mr. Willis noticed that students were more prepared for their work on each unit of instruction and had more to say in class discussions. He also noticed higher grades on tests. He excitedly reported that William came in after school and asked whether he could have some blank TRIMS Learning Sheets so he could survey his social studies textbook, because he wanted to get a better grade in social studies.

Who Can Provide Additional Information?

Coordinator of Training
Center for Research on Learning
University of Kansas
3061 Dole Center
Lawrence, KS 66045
785/864-4780
Website: www.ku-crl.org

What Other Information Is Available?

Deshler, D. D., Schumaker, J. B., & McKnight, P. (1997). *The survey routine.* Lawrence: Center for Research on Learning, University of Kansas.

Deshler, D. D., Schumaker, J. B., & McKnight, P. (1999). *Effects of surveying textbook chapters on students' performance on unit tests.* Manuscript in preparation.

References

Armbruster, B. B. (1984). The problem of "inconsiderate text." In G. G. Duffy, L. R. Roehler, & J. Mason, (Eds.), *Comprehension instruction: Perspectives and suggestions* (pp. 202–217). New York: Longman.

Deshler, D. D., Schumaker, J. B., & McKnight, P. (1997). *The survey routine.* Lawrence: Center for Research on Learning, University of Kansas.

Deshler, D. D., Schumaker, J. B., & McKnight, P. (1999). *Effects of surveying textbook chapters on students' performance on unit tests.* Manuscript in preparation.

Warner, M. M., Schumaker, J. B., Alley, G. R., & Deshler, D. D. (1980). Learning disabled adolescents in public schools: Are they different from other low achievers? *Exceptional Education Quarterly, 1*(2), 27–35.

4

Selecting Alternate Materials

Bonnie Grossen
University of Oregon

The following adaptations are included in this chapter:

9. **Coherent Text Built Around Big Ideas** *(Carnine, Crawford, Harniss, & Hollenbeck).*

10. **Reasoning and Writing** *(Engelmann, Silbert, & Grossen).*

11. **Science Videodisc Media** *(Engelmann, Hofmeister, & Carnine).*

12. **Connecting Math Concepts** *(Engelmann, Carnine, Kelly, & Engelmann) and Core Concepts Videodisc Programs (Engelmann, Hofmeister, & Carnine).*

Sometimes the existing curricular materials are so poorly designed or so difficult to use that the time and resources required to alter them or to provide teacher guidance in their use makes their adaptation a frustrating and ineffective option. When this level of frustration is reached, the design of the existing materials is deemed inappropriate and a new set should be selected. The teacher must seek out alternative materials that are more sensitive to the needs of students with disabilities. In other words, materials must be selected that are inherently designed to accommodate special learning needs. These materials build adaptations into the design of the curricular material that are more pervasive and coherent than those that can be achieved by modifying the existing curriculum.

The National Center to Improve the Tools of Educators (NCITE) has identified six adaptation principles that are particularly powerful if

---

built into the design of the instruction (Kame'enui & Carnine, 1998). These principles are discussed at length in the first volume of this series (*Toward Successful Inclusion of Students with Disabilities: The Architecture of Instruction* by Edward J. Kame'enui and Deborah C. Simmons, 1999). Table 3 notes the qualities of each of these six design considerations and provides brief examples taken from *Understanding U.S. History* (Carnine, Crawford, Harniss, Hollenbeck, & Steely, 1999). Further elaboration follows. Figure 24 provides a rubric for identifying and selecting curricular materials that are designed with these six principles in mind.

The following sections (Adaptations 9 through 12) provide more detailed examples of how the use of instructional tools designed around these six principles have accommodated students with disabilities while accelerating the performance of the classroom group as a whole. Although many teachers focus on the nature of a tool (e.g., textbook versus computer), NCITE's adaptations focus not so much on the medium as on the design of the instruction. An early study comparing instruction delivered via dynamic video as opposed to teacher-directed delivery found that the medium did not make a difference in the instructional effectiveness of these adaptations (Hasselbring et al., 1988). Another carefully designed study comparing the same instructional design as the one used in Hasselbring and colleagues' (1988) study with a more traditional, topical design, both delivered via the same dynamic video medium, found that the design of the instruction was a critical factor in the success of many students (Woodward, 1994). Thus, the design of the instruction, not the delivery medium, is the critical factor for success.

References

Carnine, D., Crawford, D., Harness, M., Hollenbeck, K., & Steely, D. (1999). *Understanding U.S. history Volume 1—Through 1914.* Eugene: University of Oregon.

Hasselbring, T., Sherwood, R., Bransford, J., Fleenor, K., Griffith, D., & Goin, L. (1988). An evaluation of level-one instructional videodisc program. *Journal of Educational Technology Systems, 16,* 151–169.

Kame'enui, E., & Carnine, D. (1998). *Effective teaching strategies that accommodate diverse learners.* Columbus, OH: Merrill.

Kame'enui, E. J., & Simmons, D. C. (1999). *Toward successful inclusion of students with disabilities: The architecture of instruction.* (ERIC/OSEP Mini-Library on Adapting Curricular Materials. *Volume 1: An overview of materials adaptations.*) Reston, VA: The Council for Exceptional Children.

TABLE 3
Principles of Effective Instructional Design

NCITE's Design Considerations	*Example from Understanding U.S. History*
Big Ideas are the focus of instruction. Big ideas are concepts and principles that apply to a wide range of examples and situations. Big ideas enable students to learn more in less time.	The major *big idea* is the problem–solution–effect pattern of history.
Conspicuous Strategies show the specific steps that lead to solving complex problems.	Students are explicitly shown how to use the problem–solution–effect graphic organizer to analyze the cause for a sequence of events in history, to generate "what-if" alternatives, and to develop informed opinions regarding current social problems.
Background Knowledge is pretaught.	*Essential vocabulary* is carefully taught.
Mediated Scaffolding provides personal guidance, assistance, and support that is faded over time.	The text first illustrates the big idea, showing how different Native American cultures solved the problem of survival in their different environments. Then students identify the components of the problem–solution–effect big idea themselves as they study later historical events. Finally, students apply the problem–solution–effect analysis to current social problems.
Judicious Review requires students to draw upon and apply previously learned knowledge over time.	The big idea is continuously reviewed throughout the entire study of history.
New knowledge is *Strategically Integrated* with old knowledge.	The problem–solution–effect big idea provides a framework for organizing and integrating all historical events as students study them.

FIGURE 24
Identifying and Selecting Curricular Materials
Based on the Six Curricular Design Principles

MATERIALS EVALUATION PROCESS AND SCORING CRITERIA

Phase 1: Select a group of finalist programs for closer evaluation.

Compare the student assignments at the beginning of a level with those at the end.

- Is the assumed competence at the beginning of the program appropriate for the lowest student who will be in the program?
- Are the expectations at the end of the program worthwhile goals?
- Do the goals of the curriculum material match the goals of the school?

(Go on to Phase 2 to review only those programs that meet all the Phase 1 criteria.)

Phase 2: Carefully evaluate the finalist programs according to research-based criteria.

The criteria below are designed to answer the question, *"How likely is the program to enable all students to reach the program goals?"*

I. BIG IDEAS
1. Is the number of objectives reasonable for diverse learners?
2. Does the instructional yield seem commensurate with the learning time?

II. CONSPICUOUS STRATEGIES
3. Are the steps for a strategy clear and complete?
4. Will the strategy consistently apply to all relevant problems without fail? (Test: Is there any way a student could apply the strategy correctly yet get the wrong answer?)
5. Are the strategies powerful? Do they apply to a wide range of problems, or must they be modified or unlearned in later work?
6. Do the example sets disallow misrules? (Are they sufficient in range? Are important discriminations made conspicuous?) (Misrules occur when students can get the correct answer to a problem but for the wrong reason [e.g., predictability], or can get an answer to a problem incorrect based on the teacher's demonstration or range of examples.)

III. MEDIATED SCAFFOLDING
7. Are prompts, cues, templates, consistent sentence sequences, and so on used to scaffold initial instruction? (Either the teacher's wording, the item form, or both may provide scaffolds.)
8. Does the teacher's guide give guidelines for correcting student errors during the lesson?
9. Are scaffolds progressively removed until each student is finally expected to do the work without the help of the teacher or other students? Has enough practice been provided to make this expectation reasonable?

Phase 2 (Continued)

10. Do the complex tasks require only the use of strategies and components that have been taught?
11. Does the text give guidelines for checking student performance at the end of a lesson or group of lessons? (Does the text indicate how the teacher should restore scaffolding if the instruction moved too quickly for some students?)

IV. STRATEGIC INTEGRATION

12. Is new information presented one concept or skill at a time?
13. Are component skills integrated and applied in progressively more complex tasks?
14. Are the component skills well established prior to integration into the more complex tasks? (Most skills require more than 2 days of practice following initial instruction in the component to become well established.)

V. PRIMED BACKGROUND KNOWLEDGE

15. Are new concepts introduced using familiar vocabulary?
16. Is new vocabulary introduced using familiar concepts?
17. Are component skills taught prior to instruction in the complex tasks they are part of?

    For example, in mathematics:

    - Does counting occur prior to adding?
    - Are fractions taught prior to decimals?
    - Are decimals taught prior to counting money?
    - Are fractions taught prior to measurement?
    - Is a strategy for finding a common multiple taught prior to adding or subtracting fractions with unlike denominators?

VI. JUDICIOUS REVIEW

18. How often does a set of mixed problem types (cumulative review) occur?

    Daily = highest score
    Lower frequency = lower score

19. Is practice distributed over time? (Look for the introduction of a topic that is not necessarily a component of other skills. Are students periodically required to use skills after instruction in the topic is finished?)

Phase 3: Gather student performance data for each finalist program.

Review and compare performance data regarding effectiveness of the programs. Ask the publisher for names of schools using each program. Inquire regarding changes in school performance levels when the school began using the program.

continues

FIGURE 24 *(Continued)*

Phase 4: Carefully evaluate the finalist programs according to research-based criteria. Award points as follows:

2 = elaborated/well met   0 = questionable
1 = mentioned/adequate   −1 = inaccurate/inadequate

Write the name of each finalist program at the top of a column.

TOTAL					
BIG IDEAS 1. Number of objectives reasonable. 2. Efficiency?					
CONSPICUOUS STRATEGIES 3. Clear and complete? 4. Strategies apply consistently? 5. Strategies powerful? 6. Misrule prevention?					
MEDIATED SCAFFOLDING 7. Evidence of prompts and other scaffolds in initial instruction? 8. Guidelines for correcting student errors? 9. Progession to independent work? 10. Complex tasks use only pretaught strategies? 11. Tests and remediation?					
STRATEGIC INTEGRATION 12. One concept at a time? 13. Component skills integrated into complex tasks? 14. Component skills well established prior to complex tasks?					
PRIMED BACKGROUND KNOWLEDGE 15. New concepts with familiar vocabulary? 16. New vocabulary with familiar concepts? 17. Component skills prior to complex tasks?					
JUDICIOUS REVIEW 18. Cumulative? (Daily = highest score; Lower frequency = lower score) 19. Distributed over time?					

Woodward, J. (1994). Effects of curriculum discourse style on eighth graders' recall and problem solving in earth science. *The Elementary School Journal, 94,* 299–314.

9. Coherent Text Built Around Big Ideas

In U.S. history classes, the problems of students with disabilities are often shared by other students as well. These problems result largely from "inconsiderate" texts (Armbruster, 1984)—that is, texts that suffer from incoherence, an overload of facts, and other design problems that make comprehension difficult for some students. The reading difficulties of students with disabilities are compounded in these texts by the long strings of dates and events that usually obfuscate the major concepts of history. For example, the traditional approach to teaching the causes of the Revolutionary War focuses on a series of acts imposed on the colonies by the British (e.g., the Wool Act, the Hat Act, the Iron Act, the Navigation Acts, the Sugar Act, the Stamp Act).

The Adaptation

In contrast, Carmine, Crawford, Hollenbeck, and Harniss (1995) identified a major big idea in history—a problem–solution–effect pattern—around which they designed a history text. Using this big idea to understand history, students learn that people are primarily reactive, coming up with solutions that have effects that lead to further problems.

For example, the American Revolution was a result of the way England tried to solve some of its economic problems. During the mid-1700s, England needed to import raw materials for industries that often did not show a profit; moreover, the English government had debts from the French and Indian War. England's solution to these economic problems was to pass a number of revenue-producing laws that required the colonists to buy manufactured goods from England, sell raw materials only to England, and pay taxes on many items brought into the colonies. The effects of these laws were that the colonists smuggled goods in and out of the country and boycotted the purchase of some English goods, thereby producing the conflict that eventually led to war.

Most problems of history are similar in that they involve economics, although religious freedom or human rights may also be involved. The solutions can also be limited to several categories: fighting, moving, inventing, accommodating, or tolerating. The limited number of causes and solutions makes it possible to teach all students the problem–solution pattern in history and guide them in applying it to better understand problems between social groups. As Kinder and Bursuck (1991) pointed out:

> Consider the invention of the cotton gin. Generally, the isolated fact that Eli Whitney invented the cotton gin is taught; however, the need for the cotton gin at that time and the historical effects of that invention usually are not made clear. The problem–solution–effect analysis showed these causal connections. Unlike the cotton grown in Egypt, most of the cotton grown in the southern United States was short-staple cotton. The short fibers made it difficult and expensive to remove the seeds—another economically based problem. The solution was Eli Whitney's machine that removed the seeds. The effect was that much more cotton could be cleaned in a day, farmers could sell more cotton, and they were in turn motivated to grow more cotton, which ultimately increased the need for slaves. (p. 273)

Figure 25 displays the graphic organizer for the problem–solution–effect pattern. This organizer also is useful in teaching multiple perspectives. For example, England's solutions to its economic problems were actually problems for the colonies. With multiple perspectives, students learn that certain events represent a solution for one group, but at the same time are a problem for another group.

Looking at the bigger picture of history also reveals significant shifts in the patterns of human response to problems. For example, most history books present a list of new discoveries made during the Enlightenment without indicating clearly that this type of problem solving was a rather sudden shift from when humans relied more on worship and religious faith as solutions. In this case, people's faith was severely shaken by the discovery that the Earth orbited around the sun rather than being positioned in the center of the universe and, therefore, possibly was not the center of God's attention and personal engagement. Rather than relying entirely on God, humans began to rely more on themselves to solve their problems. An understanding of the problem–solution–effect big idea enables students to better grapple with social problems.

Another built-in accommodation in the adapted text is strategically placed questions to make conspicuous the way that students with good comprehension skills constantly interact with text. Questions are placed after each paragraph rather than at the end of the chapter. Necessary background vocabulary is carefully taught. The text

FIGURE 25
Problem–Solution–Effect

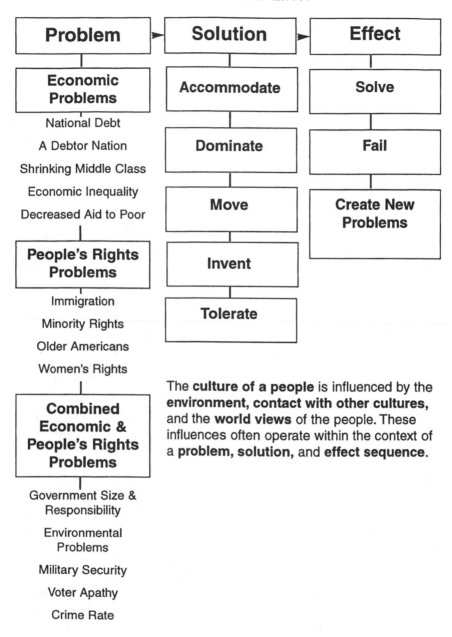

Problem	Solution	Effect

Economic Problems — **Accommodate** — **Solve**

National Debt

A Debtor Nation — **Dominate** — **Fail**

Shrinking Middle Class

Economic Inequality — **Move** — **Create New Problems**

Decreased Aid to Poor

People's Rights Problems — **Invent**

Immigration

Minority Rights — **Tolerate**

Older Americans

Women's Rights

Combined Economic & People's Rights Problems

Government Size & Responsibility

Environmental Problems

Military Security

Voter Apathy

Crime Rate

The **culture of a people** is influenced by the **environment, contact with other cultures,** and the **world views** of the people. These influences often operate within the context of a **problem, solution,** and **effect sequence.**

provides model answers for core test questions and multiple opportunities for students to practice these responses. In addition, supplemental and challenge questions are provided for more advanced learners. Judicious review occurs with the repeated application of the big idea throughout the scope of the text, until any student can generalize the use of the problem–solution–effect analysis to interpret current events and relate them to history.

What Research Backs It Up?

Five intervention studies to date have evaluated the effects of the use of the history text with built-in accommodations for the performance of students with disabilities (Carnine, Caros, Crawford, Hollenbeck, & Harniss, 1996).

Two field studies compared the effects of the *Understanding U.S. History* text designed according to NCITE's six principles with a theme-driven social studies/language arts integrated class that used published mainstream texts. The NCITE text resulted in better writing scores ($n = 104$) and better content knowledge ($n = 81$) as indicated by short-answer tests for general education students. The design features accelerated the learning for these students.

A third study evaluated the effects on written responses to a primary source prompt for different types of students: (a) diverse (i.e., either receiving special education services or receiving counseling services as highly at risk), (b) middle, and (c) high (i.e., the best students academically). Instruction was delivered to these types of students in the same instructional setting. Results showed no significant differences between the groups, indicating that the design features incorporated into the text do accommodate diverse academic levels of students. (The scores for all three groups were reasonably high.)

A fourth study evaluated the effects of history taught with the NCITE text versus the district-adopted text on the learning of students with disabilities. The use of the NCITE text resulted in better performance on measures of content knowledge and significantly better on-task behavior and participation, as indicated by a greater number of questions answered correctly in class.

A fifth study indicated that students' rate of learning vocabulary doubled using the procedures in the NCITE text.

We recently surveyed seven teachers who used the problem–solution–effect analysis with a world history text that had not been rewritten to make this pattern explicit throughout the events of history. These teachers all strongly agreed that using a text written to incorporate the problem–solution–effect text structure in addition to the graphic organizer would be more effective.

What Does It Look Like in Practice?

Clarissa has a learning disability in basic reading and generally has not succeeded in general education classes that rely heavily on a textbook. Not only does Clarissa have difficulty passing the classes, but she also becomes a behavior problem. However, Clarissa is passing Mrs. Frederick's U.S. history class. Even though the class receives a lot of assignments from the text, Clarissa is able to do these satisfactorily.

When new material is introduced, the class reads orally a paragraph at a time and then answers the question in the text that follows the paragraph. Clarissa listens to other students read while she follows along in her book. She also gets a turn to read now and then. Mrs. Frederick calls on Clarissa frequently to answer questions. From this oral work—reading in small chunks, answering questions, and discussing relationships as the class moves through the material—the vocabulary study that occurs every day for 5 to 10 minutes, the practice essays, and other accommodating design features—she is able to do well on the tests.

Challenge questions are available on the tests for more advanced students who want to get an A. Clarissa tries the challenge questions sometimes also. With the knowledge she gains, she is able to analyze current events with the rest of the class and offer ideas for solutions for current social conflicts.

She is able to explain major events in history in terms of the causes and the chain of events leading up to these turning points in history. Because she is able to contribute to the class in a meaningful way, she is no longer the behavior problem she once was in classes making heavy use of a textbook. Here is the text of her essay response to a primary source document prompt about the American Revolutionary War, with spelling errors removed:

> *To fully explain what you wish to know I will start from the beginning. The Revolutionary War came about because of, you guessed it, money. Britain needed money and finances to sustain their armies and navies. They lost a lot of money because of the French and Native American War over the Ohio Valley. They needed money so they taxed the colonists. The first big tax was the Navigation Acts which controlled trade. These acts were eventually repealed because of smugglers! There were several acts. The major ones were the Townshend Act, Sugar Acts, and Stamp Act. All were broken through some way or another, whether smugglers or boycotting or even one time a ship was burned and everybody knows the Boston Tea Party. Well, King George was mad at the colonists for rebelling so he made laws to punish. The baddest*

thing that these laws did was close the Boston Harbor! The Second Continental Congress wished to stop bad deeds with Britain and the King so they wrote the Olive Branch Petition and King George didn't even read it. Instead he wrote the Proclamation of Rebellion.

Britain had heard that in Concord a militia was stockpiling ammunition, canons, and guns. British troops were sent to take the guns and stockpiled goods. That is when Paul Revere and others went riding to warn towns. Paul Revere rode through Lexington crying, "the British are coming." That morning the militia gathered on Lexington Green when the British came. The Battle of Lexington Concord happened. British won. But when they came to Concord they could not find but very few weapons and stockpiled goods.

Obviously, Clarissa has learned a lot about American history and is eager to convey her knowledge.

What Other Information Is Available?

For sample copies or to order the history books Volumes 1 and 2 contact:

Chris Davis
University of Oregon Bookstore Warehouse
Attention: Mail Order Dept.
462 East 8th
Eugene, OR 97401
541/345-8805 or 1-800-352-1733
Fax: 541/346-3516

Grossen, B., & Carnine, D. (1992). Translating research on text structure into classroom practice. *TEACHING Exceptional Children*, 24(4), 48–53.

References

Armbruster, B. (1984). The problem of "inconsiderate text." In G. G. Duffy, L. R. Roehler, & J. Mason (Eds.), *Comprehension instruction* (pp. 207–217). New York; Longman.

Carnine. D., Caros, J., Crawford, D., Hollenbeck, K., & Harniss, M. (1996). Designing effective U.S. history curricula for all students. In J. Brophy (Ed.), *Sixth Handbook on Research on Teaching. Advances in Research on Teaching* (Vol. 6, pp. 207–256). Greenwich, CT: JAI.

Carnine, D., Crawford, D., Harniss. M., & Hollenbeck, K. (1995). *Understanding U.S. history.* Eugene: University of Oregon.

Kinder, D., & Bursuck, W. (1991). The search for a unified social studies curriculum: Does history really repeat itself? *Journal of Learning Disabilities, 24,* 270–75.

10. Reasoning and Writing

Many assume that inquiry (discovery) teaching methods are the best way to teach students strategies for constructing new knowledge. While this may be true for students who already possess some inquiry skills, students who lack these skills have no way to get them. Kuhn (1993) found that 60% of the general adult population cannot apply some of the most basic principles of reasoning and hypothesis testing. This figure undoubtedly includes persons with disabilities as well as those with poor reasoning skills. This adaptation was developed to provide teachers an alternative way to teach inquiry skills, among other important skills, for using evidence to review opinions, test hypotheses, and so on.

The Adaptation

The *Reasoning and Writing* program (Englemann & Grossen, 1996) is a textbook with teacher presentation manual that applies the six design principles to develop rigorous skills in logic and inquiry. The program scaffolds students' writing development through the use of graphic organizers that illustrate the cognitive structures to be used. The cognitive structures include comparing/contrasting, identifying invalid conclusions (e.g., false cause), drawing analogies, and using evidence to support conclusions, among many others.

What Research Backs It Up?

A series of studies have evaluated specific features of the design of the instruction to teach reasoning. Some of the studies used a computer medium to deliver the instruction so that teaching variables could be tightly controlled. The first study compared the use of explicit instruction in logic with nonexplicit instruction. The results indicated that high-school students with learning disabilities who received the explicit instruction could achieve a mean score on logic critiquing that exceeded the mean score of university students in a teacher-training course (Collins & Carnine, 1988).

Grossen and Carnine (1990) found that a written response requiring a deeper level of processing had stronger effects than a simple multiple-choice selection procedure. In this study, students with disabilities matched the performance of high-school students classified as talented and gifted on tasks requiring critical thinking. (See Grossen & Carnine, 1996, for a description of some of these tasks and details regarding the performance of students with disabilities.)

Grossen, Lee, and Johnston (1995) compared the effects of instruction in an algorithmic strategy for logical thinking with instruction that involved practice working naturalistic logic problems. The algorithmic strategy produced stronger results, not only for students with disabilities but even more so for the general education students learning in the same classroom environment.

These specific research findings were incorporated into the design of the comprehensive textbook program for teaching reasoning and writing (Engelmann & Grossen, 1996). Data from the implementation of this program have shown an increase on the Test of Written Language (Hammill & Larsen, 1996) of more than two standard deviations in one year in general education classrooms.

What Does It Look Like in Practice?

Annette has a learning disability in writing and comprehension. Her compositions are generally very short and not very informative. She was placed in a mainstream eighth-grade writing class where *Reasoning and Writing* was used as the core program of instruction. Each time the class learned a new writing form, they followed an outline diagram, which graphically represented the thinking process they were expected to use and provided them with many of the routine words that made their essays sound "smart."

Annette was amazed at how good her critiques sounded. She was eager to read them in class. She found she had to think hard when she did these activities, but somehow the program always seemed to prepare her for the next, more difficult task. She noticed, for example, that the thinking process they had been using to test rules was the same process they used to figure out whether or not a conclusion was valid.

Figures 26 through 28 illustrate samples from the sequence of tasks Annette completed to learn how to construct knowledge. Figure 26 is the first type of task in this series. Annette had to figure out what was in the mystery box and write a paragraph describing her thinking process. The outline diagram provided a template for her paragraph. The icons graphically represented the type of thinking involved. Annette had already learned that the trapezoid prompted a summary statement, or topic sentence. The boxes illustrated the stepwise nature

FIGURE 26

Follow the outline diagram to explain how you identified the mystery object.

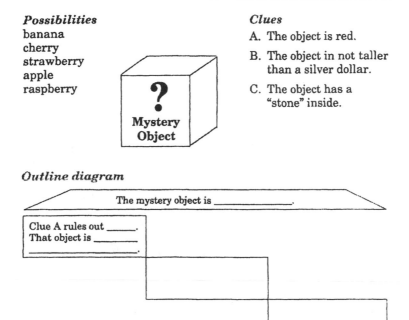

Possibilities
banana
cherry
strawberry
apple
raspberry

Clues
A. The object is red.

B. The object in not taller than a silver dollar.

C. The object has a "stone" inside.

Outline diagram

The mystery object is _____.

Clue A rules out _____.
That object is _____
_____.

The only remaining possibility is _____.

of the ruling-out process used in constructing knowledge. And finally, another trapezoid indicated a concluding sentence. To figure out the mystery object, Annette read the first clue, "The object is red," and then reviewed the possibilities. Following the outline diagram, she wrote, "Clue A rules out the banana. That object is not red," and so on.

This thinking strategy has wide application. Having worked through several tasks like the one shown in Figure 26, Annette encountered the task shown in Figure 27, which guided her in applying the ruling-out process to a shopping problem: "Henry needs a jacket and has several requirements." In this scenario there is a jacket that meets his requirements. In other activities, Annette encountered scenarios where no option met the all the requirements, so she had to weigh the alternatives and choose the best option.

FIGURE 27

Part A	Follow the outline diagram to write how you selected the best jacket for Henry.

Henry's requirements

1. The jacket must cost less than $200.00.
2. The jacket must be washable.
3. The jacket must offer superior protection against the cold.
4. The jacket must weigh no more than 4 pounds.

Facts

Jacket	Stormbuster	Windblaster	Leader	King Kold	Wilderness
Price	$179.00	$187.99	$156.00	$206.00	$187.00
Weight	4 lb.	3 lb. 2 oz.	2 lb. 8 oz.	3 lb. 7 oz	4 lb. 3 oz.
Protection against cold	superior	superior	good	superior	superior
Cleaning	washable	dry clean only	washable	washable	washable

Outline diagram

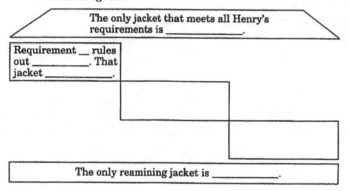

Annette and all the other students in the class used this same ruling-out process for many other kinds of applications. They used it to select the best plan for accomplishing a goal, such as learning how to ride a horse when a person lives in the city, has no money, and has no horse.

The ruling-out process also represents the fundamental thinking involved in setting up and interpreting the outcomes of scientific experiments. Figure 28 illustrates a problem requiring an experiment before a conclusion can be made. Not all the possible explanations for an observation have been ruled out. Annette described a short experiment and then described how to interpret the data, depending on how

FIGURE 28

Follow the outline diagram to explain about the problem with Sam's test.

Sam's test

Sam did an experiment with maple seeds. He planted 600 seeds at a depth of one-half inch below the surface of the dirt. He controlled the temperature of the soil so it was above 60 degrees Fahrenheit. Nearly all the seeds sprouted.

He planted another batch of seeds two inches deep. He put them in a place that had a temperature that was less than 60 degrees. Almost none of those seeds sprouted.

Sam's conclusion

A temperature above 60 degrees causes the seeds to sprout.

Outline diagram

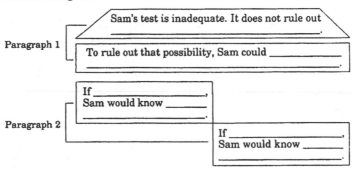

the experiment turned out. One of the remaining possible explanations for the observation would be ruled out in this experiment.

The outline diagrams shown in Figures 26 through 28 provide students with a clear model of the wording and thinking processes involved. Later these prompts are faded after students have internalized the thinking patterns and are able to work successfully without the prompts (mediated scaffolding).

What Other Information Is Available?

For more information or to order *Reasoning and Writing* contact Science Research Associates, 1-888-772-4543.

Collins, M., Carnine, D., & Gersten, R. (1987). Elaborated corrective feedback and the acquisition of reasoning skills: a study of computer-assisted instruction. *Exceptional Children, 54,* 254–262.

Kame'enui, E., & Carnine, D. (1998). *Effective teaching strategies that accommodate diverse learners.* Columbus, OH: Merrill.

References

Collins, M., & Carnine, D. (1988). Evaluating the field test revision process by comparing two versions of a reasoning skills CAI program. *Journal of Learning Disabilities, 21,* 375–379.

Englemann, S., & Grossman, B. (1996). *Reasoning and writing, levels E & F.* Columbus, OH: Science Research Associates.

Grossen, B., & Carnine, D. (1990). Diagramming a logic strategy: Effects on difficult problem types and transfer. *Learning Disability Quarterly, 13,* 168–182.

Grossen, B., & Carnine, D. (1996). Considerate instruction helps students with disabilities achieve world class standards. *TEACHING Exceptional Children, 28*(4), 77–81.

Grossen, B., Lee, C., & Johnston, D. (1995). A comparison of the effects of direct instruction in reasoning with constructivism on deductive reasoning. In A. Deffenbaugh, G. Sugai, & G. Tindal (Eds.), *The Oregon Conference 1995* [Monograph] (pp. 253–273). Eugene: College of Education, University of Oregon.

Hammill, D., & Larsen, S. (1996).Test of Written Language. Austin, TX: Pro-Ed.

Kuhn, D. (1993). Science as argument: Implications for teaching and learning scientific thinking. *Science Education, 77,* 319–337.

11. Science Videodisc Media

Because academic expectations in science instruction are so great, students with disabilities are often excluded. To facilitate inclusion, the goals of the class can be watered down. However, the knowledge base in the science-related fields is expanding so rapidly that avoidance tactics such as postponing the introduction of content will ultimately deny students in general, as well as students with disabilities, access to science-related fields.

The Adaptation

A videodisc curriculum with built-in accommodations for diverse learners was developed to communicate rigorous earth science knowledge in a user-friendly manner (Core Concepts, 1987). The design of the videodisc program exemplifies the features of instructional design identified as critical in accommodating the needs of diverse learners (Grossen, Romance, & Vitale, 1997; Kame'enui & Carnine, 1998).

The curriculum is organized around the big idea of convection, instead of the usual organization into declarative topics: the solid earth (geology), the atmosphere (meteorology), and the ocean (oceanography). The principle of convection provides the underlying explanation for most of the dynamic phenomena occurring in these three declarative topic areas. Plate tectonics, earthquakes, volcanoes, and the formation of mountains are all a result of convection in the mantle. The dynamics of the atmosphere that cause changing weather are influenced by global and local convection patterns. Similarly, the ocean currents, thermo-haline circulation, and coastal upwelling are influenced by global and local convection. The interaction of these phenomena in the earth and the atmosphere result in the rock cycle, weathering, and changes in land forms. The interaction of these phenomena in the ocean and in the atmosphere result in the water cycle, wind-driven ocean circulation, El Niño, and climate variations in general.

To gain an in-depth understanding of convection, students must fully understand the interaction of density, pressure, force, and heating and cooling. For example, students must understand that heat causes a substance to become less dense, that less dense substances move from a place of high pressure to a place of low pressure, and so on. Furthermore, a specific set of facts about the solar system, the ocean, the solid earth, and the atmosphere are essential in understanding and applying these principles. For example, students learn that the sun is the primary source of heat, that the tilt of the earth as it rotates around the sun causes changes in the amount of heat received in different areas of the earth (i.e., changing seasons), that the core of the earth is hot, that the ocean is very, very deep, and so on.

Figure 29 illustrates the core principle of convection and various related phenomena. These phenomena and many others are described in conceptual models that use words and diagrams to highlight the major concepts and the causal relationships among them. These models represent basic problem patterns students use to solve problems. These problem pattern models are presented only after key concepts in the model and the interaction of those concepts are taught.

Cognitive strategies for analyzing problems are taught conspicuously, and mediated scaffolding leads the learners to greater independence and versatility in applying these strategies in solving problems. For example, density is introduced using a dot in a cube to represent 1 gram of weight. Two cubes with differing numbers of dots are illustrated, and students are asked which is more dense. Then figures of different sizes are shown (see Figure 30). The program shows students

FIGURE 29

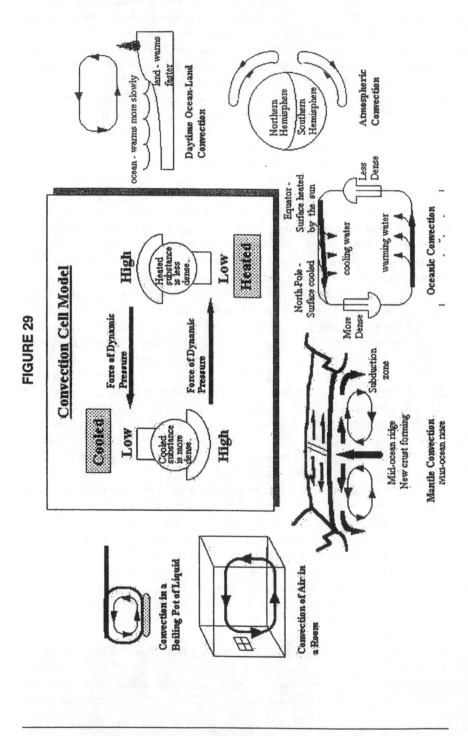

Convection Cell Model

Cooled — Low — Cooled substance is more dense. — High

Force of Dynamic Pressure

Force of Dynamic Pressure

Heated substance is less dense. — High — Low — Heated

Daytime Ocean-Land Convection

ocean - warms more slowly

land - warms faster

Atmospheric Convection

Northern Hemisphere

Southern Hemisphere

Convection in a Boiling Pot of Liquid

Convection of Air in a Room

Mantle Convection
Mid-ocean ridge

Mid-ocean ridge
New crust forming

Subduction zone

Oceanic Convection

Equator - Surface heated by the sun

North Pole - Surface cooled

cooling water

warming water

Less Dense

More Dense

FIGURE 30

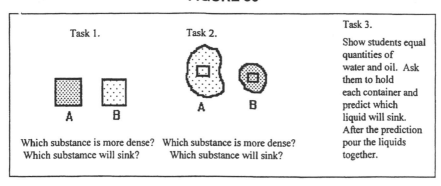

Task 1.

Which substance is more dense?
Which substamce will sink?

Task 2.

Which substance is more dense?
Which substance will sink?

Task 3.

Show students equal quantities of water and oil. Ask them to hold each container and predict which liquid will sink. After the prediction pour the liquids together.

how to think about density by placing empty cubes over equal-size segments of the objects. By looking at the number of dots in the cube, students can tell that substance B is more dense than substance A, although blob B is smaller. Later, real objects illustrate the rule that if a substance is more dense than the medium containing it, it will sink. If the substance is less dense, it will rise or float.

Other conceptual models illustrate convection as an explanation for phenomena from the diverse areas of geology, oceanography, and meteorology, as alluded to in Figure 29. Each of these models establishes a problem pattern. These models are not unrelated; they form part of a unified, structured convection.

Besides organizing the content differently from a traditional textbook, the presentation techniques themselves are different in the videodisc program. The presentation emphasizes frequent oral and written response, frequent assessment and feedback, and dynamic presentation of information.

The videodisc program consists of six 5-lesson units, including six in-program tests, quizzes, and review and remedial exercises. In each lesson (approximately 45 minutes long), two or more concepts are taught using dynamic video selections and fairly short explanations followed by application items. Each of the concepts is taught to a criterion of performance, then tested before the next lesson. Every five lessons, students work in cooperative groups to solve challenging problems requiring them to apply the concepts they have learned.

What Research Backs It Up?

Several intervention studies have evaluated the effectiveness of the videodisc curricula in teaching students with disabilities. Niedelmann (1992) found that the mean score of students with disabilities learning from the videodisc program matched the mean score of general education students learning from a standard science textbook in a class that emphasized frequent hands-on labs.

Muthukrishna, Carnine, Grossen, and Miller (1993) found that in interviews the students with disabilities demonstrated a scientific understanding of principles of science that Harvard graduates frequently misunderstood, according to filmed interviews by Schneps (1987). These students with disabilities also indicated a greater interest in taking more science classes in the future.

Grossen, Lee, and Carnine (1999) compared the videodisc program to a constructivist intervention and found that the videodisc program resulted in significantly more sound understandings and significantly fewer misconceptions than the constructivist intervention. Mastery of concepts and problem solving was also better for the videodisc group. A group of students with disabilities were included in only the videodisc treatment. These students also scored more sound understandings and fewer misconceptions than the general education students in the constructivist treatment. (Recall from the introduction that Hasselbring et al., 1988, and Woodward, 1994, showed that the instructional design, not the videodisc medium, is the relevant factor explaining the positive effects of these curricular materials.)

What Does It Look Like in Practice?

Rosa, who had a learning disability in the area of reading, had never taken much of an interest in science because she had difficulty passing tests in her science class and came to view the science classes as a punishment. Nevertheless, her new videodisc class was different. She learned the first day that she had to pay attention because if she didn't the teacher would repeat the segment. After she watched the first 2-minute segment, she found she could answer the questions that were on the video screen. She was surprised to find that when she listened, she could answer all the questions without any help. Then the next segment was a little longer. What she had learned in the first explanation helped her understand the next. The explanations were so clear, and her poor reading did not cause her the usual problems because she did not have to read to learn.

She was also surprised to see that she did not seem to forget very much, because every day the class was expected to use what they had learned the day before to figure out more and more difficult things. By the ninth lesson, she understood something called *convection*, which explained to her the relationship of heat to weather-related events, the formation of mountains, the ocean currents, and so on. When the tests came, Rosa got high grades. Figure 31 shows her answer to a question

FIGURE 31

Mountains are formed 2 ways. I know from science class that mid-ocean ridges that is when the eaths plates are moving apart by convection in the mantle and let lava come up and make a mountain. The second way that mountains are formed is by the earths plates going on top of each other by the opposite convection of the mid-ocean ridges in the mantle. Also mid-ocean ridges are usualy found at the bottom of the ocean and subduction zones (the second one) are most- ly found on the coast of the Picific ocean.

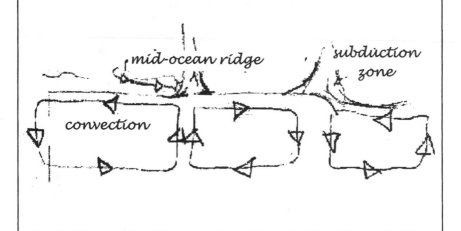

asking her to explain how mountains form. One night she explained to her parents why the fishing was so good on the Pacific coast. Her dad loved to fish, but he didn't know how ocean upwelling worked. Rosa decided that she was actually pretty good in science and decided to take more science in high school.

When she and her classmates got to high school, many of them ended up in the same class. The high school teacher was amazed at what they knew. The teacher said he had never seen a class with so much understanding of science. Rosa felt proud to be one of those smart students.

Who Can Provide Additional Information?

BFA Educational Media
2349 Chaffee Drive
St. Louis, MO 63146
314/569-0211 or 1-800-221-1274

What Other Information Is Available?

Grossen, B., Romance, N., & Vitale, M. (1994). Science: Educational tools for diverse learners. *School Psychology Review, 23,* 442–468.

Burke, M., Hagan, S., & Grossen, B. (1998). What curricular designs and strategies accommodate diverse learners? *TEACHING Exceptional Children, 31*(1), 34–38.

Burke, M., Coulter, G., & Grossen, B. (1997). Instructional design and videodisc technology: A promising vehicle for improving academic performance in students with emotional and behavior disorders. In R. E. Schmid & W. Evan (Eds.), *Curriculum and instructional practices for students with emotional and behavioral disorders* (pp. 21–28). Reston, VA: Council for Children with Behavior Disorders, The Council for Exceptional Children.

References

Core Concepts. (1987). *Core concepts in earth science.* [Videodisc program]. St. Louis: Phoenix Film BFA.

Grossen, B., Romance, N., & Vitale, M. (1998). Effective strategies for teaching science. In E. Kame'enui & D. Carnine (Eds.), *Effective teaching strategies that accommodate diverse learners* (pp. 113–137). Columbus, OH: Merrill.

Grossen, B., Lee, C., & Carnine, D. (1999). The effects of considerate expository instruction and constructivist instruction on middle-school students' achievement and problem solving in earth science. [Technical report No. 100]. Eugene: National Center to Improve the Tools of Educators, University of Oregon.

Hasselbring, T., Sherwood, R., Bransford, J., Fleenor, K., Griffith, D., & Goin, L. (1988). An evaluation of level-one instructional videodisc program. *Journal of Educational Technology Systems, 16,* 151–169.

Kame'enui, E., & Carnine, D. (1998). *Effective teaching strategies that accommodate diverse learners.* Columbus, OH: Merrill.

Muthukrishna, A., Carnine, D., Grossen, B., & Miller, S. (1993). Children's alternative frameworks: Should they be directly addressed in science instruction? *Journal of Research in Science Teaching, 30,* 233–248.

Niedelmann, M. (1992). Problem solving and transfer. In D. Carnine & E. Kame'enui (Eds.), *Higher order thinking: Designing curriculum for mainstreamed students* (pp. 137–156). Austin, TX: Pro-Ed.

Schneps, M. H. (Producer, Director). (1987). *A private universe* (Film). Boston: Harvard University and Smithsonian Institution.

Woodward, J. (1994). Effects of curriculum discourse style on eighth graders' recall and problem solving in earth science. *The Elementary School Journal, 94,* 299–314.

12. Connecting Math Concepts, SRA, and Core Concepts Videodisc Programs

Students with learning disabilities in mathematics often remain at the level of basic fact acquisition and computation in classes where little is expected of them. They do not move into the higher-level thinking involved in math problem solving. Because of this, they rarely have the opportunity to develop the basic number sense that would enable them to make rational quantitative judgments. This adaptation can give students opportunities to learn higher-order problem-solving skills.

The Adaptation

Several math programs with built-in accommodations for diverse learners (*Core Concepts,* 1987; Englemann et al., 1996) incorporate the six principles of instructional design for accommodating diversity: Big Ideas, Conspicuous Strategies, Mediated Scaffolding, Primed Background Knowledge, Judicious Review, and Strategic Integration (Kame'enui & Carnine, 1998).

The instruction in probability illustrates how these principles are applied in the design of *Connecting Math Concepts* (SRA, 1996). The concept of probability and a number of applications for probability build on a basic understanding of fractions. Students learn that the bottom number of a fraction tells the number of parts in each group and the top number tells how many of those parts are used. Consider a bag containing blue and white objects, for example:

The entire group comprises 9 objects. The fraction for the blue objects (in this case the "used" objects) is $\frac{6}{9}$. The fraction for white objects is $\frac{3}{9}$.

These fractions also represent the probability of pulling a blue or a white object from the bag. The closer a fraction is to 1, the greater the probability that fraction expresses. Students learn to represent members of a set as a fraction, then apply that knowledge to problems such as the following:

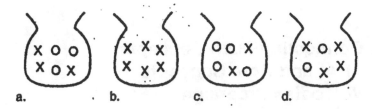

1. Which bag gives you the best chance of drawing an X?

2. Which bag gives you the second best chance of drawing an X?

3. Which bag gives you the worst chance of drawing an X?

For each bag, students write the fraction for the "winners"—in this case, Xs. The fraction closest to 1 represents the best chance, and so forth. The fractions also represent the expected outcomes for a given set of trials.

For this bag, the fraction for the Xs is $\frac{2}{6}$.

The denominator expresses the number of trials that would yield an expected outcome of 2 winners. In other words, for every 6 trials (shaking up the bag and drawing out an object without looking), one would expect to draw an X from the bag 2 times.

This statement is explored using a bag with a certain number of objects, taking trials, and recording the outcomes. For example, a bag has 7 cards, 4 of which have triangles on them. Triangles are "winners." Tallies are made for each of seven trials taken and for each time a winner is drawn.

Students then see that the expected result does not happen every time, but it does happen most of the time.

For this bag, the fraction is $\frac{6}{6}$, or 1.

A probability of 1 denotes certainty.

If you take trials for this bag, you will draw a winner every time; you cannot lose. It is the only time when you will have a winner for every trial.

Students extend what they know about probability to their knowledge of proportions. This enables them to solve problems such as:

The winners for this set are circles. How many winners would you expect if you took 42 trials?

Students first write the information provided by the composition of the set that gives the ratio of winners to trials:

$$\frac{winners}{trials} = \frac{3}{7}$$

Next, they represent the equivalent fraction that tells about 42 trials.

$$\frac{winners}{trials} \frac{3}{7} = \frac{[\ ]}{42}$$

Students complete the equivalent fraction:

$$\frac{winners}{trials} \frac{3}{7} \left(\frac{6}{6}\right) = \frac{[18]}{42}$$

They conclude that they would expect 18 winners from 42 trials.

This groundwork, expressing probability as fractions and proportions, prepares students for a variety of projects involving dice, cards, and coins. For example, in one experiment, students are presented with a bag and are told, "There are 4 cards in the bag. At least 1 of the cards is a winner (with a blue triangle on it)." Students write the ratio of the various possibilities for winners and trials:

$$\frac{1}{4} \quad \frac{2}{4} \quad \frac{3}{4} \quad \frac{4}{4}$$

Trials will be taken until 24 winners are drawn. Based on the possibilities, students construct ratio equations predicting the number of trials that would be taken to yield 24 winners:

$$\frac{winners}{trials} \frac{1}{4}\left(\frac{24}{24}\right) = \frac{24}{[96]} \qquad \frac{winners}{trials} \frac{2}{4}\left(\frac{12}{12}\right) = \frac{24}{(48)}$$

$$\frac{winners}{trials} \frac{3}{4}\left(\frac{8}{8}\right) = \frac{24}{(32)} \qquad \frac{winners}{trials} \frac{4}{4}\left(\frac{6}{6}\right) = \frac{24}{(24)}$$

The total number of trials and winners are recorded until 24 winners are drawn. The actual number of trials is then compared to the expected values for the four possibilities. Students can then accurately deduce the composition of the bag.

Thus, students have a representational framework to make sense of statements such as "The odds are 3 to 2," or "The probability of winning is 1 in 7,240,000." Students also see the power of making predictions and drawing accurate conclusions based on empirical observations.

This example illustrates how basic instruction in fractions is extended and applied to complex higher operations, such as statistics and probability, ratios and proportions.

What Research Backs It Up?

Ninth-grade students with disabilities were able to match the performance of general education students in their ability to use ratios and proportions to solve problems after learning mathematics from a math program designed around the six principles of accommodation for diverse learners (Moore & Carnine, 1989).

In another study involving fifth and sixth-graders, the sample included the full distribution of students, from those with disabilities to gifted and talented. For analysis, the instructional groups were divided into low performers (each instructional group included 5 students with disabilities in the group of 15 low performers) and high performers (each instructional group included 2 gifted and talented students in the group of 15 high performers). The low-performing half of the class learning from the accommodating program scored significantly higher than the high- performing half of the class learning from a constructivist curriculum emphasizing hands-on group learning (Grossen & Ewing, 1994).

What Does It Look Like in Practice?

Phillip had a great deal of difficulty with mathematics in elementary school. By the time he got to middle school, he was so far behind, he could not read or solve the most basic word problems. He took a videodisc math course during his first year in middle school. In that class he learned how fractions work. He learned that the bottom number was the number of parts in each group and the top number was the number of parts used. Later he learned that the bottom number was called a *denominator*. He was never confused about what the denominator was because he did not hear the word *numerator* until about 3 weeks later. When the teacher started using the word *numerator,* he was so used to calling the bottom number *denominator* that he never got them confused. His grades in that class were generally about 90%, which made him feel very good.

After that he went into one of the math classes that most of the students took, where he continued to get good grades even when the class studied difficult concepts such as ratios and proportions and probability and statistics. That class used *Connecting Math Concepts.*

It was easy for Phillip to figure out that out of 15 marbles in a bag, the chances of drawing a blue marble would be the number of blue marbles over the total number of marbles in the bag. Because he was so good with equivalent fractions, he could easily calculate the number of times a person would get a blue marble if he or she drew only 5 times, or how many times you would probably have to draw marbles to get 4 blue marbles. The way he had been taught fractions really helped him understand these operations.

Who Can Provide Additional Information?

On *Connecting Math Concepts* contact Science Research Associates:

1-888-772-4543

On *Core Concepts* programs contact:

Phoenix Film BFA
2349 Chaffee Dr.
St. Louis, MO, 63146
314/569-0211 or 1-800-221-1274

What Other Information Is Available?

Grossen, B., & Carnine, D. (1996). Considerate instruction helps students with disabilities achieve world class standards. *TEACHING Exceptional Children, 28*(4), 77–81.

References

Core Concepts. (1987). *Earth science.* St. Louis: BFA Phoenix Film.

Englemann, S. et al. (1996). *Connecting math concepts.* Columbus, OH: SRA/McGraw-Hill.

Grossen, B., & Ewing, S. (1994). Do the NCTM Teaching Standards help? Final report. *Effective School Practice, 13*(2), 79–91.

Kame'enui, E., & Carnine, D. (1998). *Effective teaching strategies that accommodate diverse learners.* Columbus, OH: Merrill.

Moore, L., & Carnine, D. (1989). Evaluating curriculum design in the context of active teaching. *Remedial and Special Education, 10*(4), 28–37.

Appendix

FIGURE A1

Checklist for Considerate Text Characteristics

Textbook Title: _____

Check each questions with a **yes** or **no**.

	YES	NO	
T			1. Does the title reflect the main idea/topic of the chapter?
R			2. Does the table of contents show relationships or organizational patterns between the unit and the current chapter?
			3. Are the headings listed in the table of contents or is there an expanded table of contents?
			4. Does the table of contents show a clear arrangement of ideas by use of one of the most common relationship structures? Check the structure used:

_____ Order	_____ Explanation
_____ Process	_____ Comparison
_____ Causality	_____ Deliberation
_____ Problem/Solution	

5. Is there a clear relationship or structure of ideas between the current chapter and the immediately preceding and the following chapters?

I

6. Is there a clearly identified introduction to the chapter?

7. Does the introduction specify chapter goals/objectives for reading?
   Are the goals/objectives: _____ Explicit (stated /listed)?
   _____ Implied (embedded)?

8. Does the introduction provide an overview of the chapter?

4. Does the introduction specify the relationship or organization of ideas/events in the chapter through use of one of the most common relationship structures? Check structure used:

_____ Order	_____ Explanation
_____ Process	_____ Comparison
_____ Causality	_____ Deliberation
_____ Problem/Solution	

10. Does the introduction state the rationale/relevance of the chapter content?
    Are the rationales/relevance statement: _____ Explicit?
    _____ Implied ?

11. Does the introduction:
    _____ review previously studied relevant material/information?
    _____ relate it to the topic of the current chapter?
    _____ explicitly state the relationship?
    _____ imply the relationship?

University of Kansas Center for Research on Learning May, 1997

M		12. Do titles of main headings and subheadings clearly reflect the main idea structure of information presented? 13. Do subheadings follow a clear sequence of information directly related to the main headings? 14. Does the author use size, shape, color, and/or placement to distinguish types of headings? 15. Are new/key vocabulary highlighted in the text? _____ In bold print or italics? _____ Listed at end of chapter, bottom of page, or margin? 16. Does the text provide _____ A definition of key terms? _____ A pronunciation guide for key terms? 17. Do graphics enhance the most important information contained in the chapter and/or related directly to headings? 18. Do graphics depict information in a succinct, easy-to-read format with instructions provided for interpretation or use of charts and graphs?
S		19. Is there a clearly identified summary? 20. Does the summary synthesize chapter contents? 21. Does the summary review chapter goals/objectives? 22. Does the summary focus student attention on the most important concepts, ideas, and information? 23. Are there chapter review/study questions? 24. Are chapter review questions based on the critical key concepts and ideas? 25. Is there a good balance among main idea, detail/fact, and critical thinking (applications, analysis, synthesis) questions?

Total number of questions answered "YES" _____

The higher the score, the more considerate and "user friendly" the textbook. The more considerate a textbook, the more likely that students will be able to use it independently. The more inconsiderate a textbook, the more teacher facilitation and intervention will be required.

University of Kansas Center for Research on Learning May, 1997

TRIMS
Strategies for Enhancing Text Problem Areas

Possible Problem Area	Teacher Strategies
Title ❑ Students are unable to paraphrase title because it contains: a) unknown vocabulary b) concepts not previously defined or studied	✔Assist students in paraphrasing title by eliciting or providing synonyms for unknown vocabulary in the title. ✔Have students change title to a question and find answer to the question in chapter introduction. ✔Assist students in dividing concept vocabulary into "word parts" to paraphrase definition of concept, e.g.: humanism = human + ism human = mankind ism = system of belief. ✔Paraphrase title for students to provide a paraphrase for them in order to give a general definition of the title/chapter topic.
Relationship ❑ Students are unable to determine he relationship of information due to a) unknown vocabulary and/or concepts in the chapter or unit titles b) lack of understanding of and/or inexperience in identifying relationship structures ❑ The order of chapters in the text does not match the order assigned by the teacher.	✔Provide practice in identifying relationships - use preceding chapters (familiar materials) as a basis for identifying relationships. ✔Provide examples of the 3 most common relationship structures used in text; elicit "real life" examples of the specific relationship; cite examples in text; have students find additional examples. ✔Name the relationship for students and provide text examples for them. ✔Direct students to analyze the order & relationship of assigned chapters. ✔Explain the relationship of chapters assigned by the teacher. ✔Compare order selected by teacher to order in the text.

University of Kansas Center for Research on Learning May, 1997

Possible Problem Area	Teacher Strategies
Introduction ❑ There is no introduction	✔Introduce the chapter to students. ✔Provide a rationale for the importance of the chapter content. ✔Review previously learned material and establish a link to chapter content.
❑ Introduction does not provide any goals/objectives for the chapter.	✔Provide students with goals/objectives for reading. ✔Continue with the survey, then have students use chapter summary, review questions, headings, etc. to develop goals/objectives for their reading.
❑ Introduction does not explicitly state (embeds) chapter goals/objectives.	✔Change the introductory sentences with implicit statements of goals/objectives to explicit statements and list on chalkboard. ✔Provide students with vocabulary usually employed in goal/objective statements (e.g. *should, will*). ✔Assist students in identifying goals/objectives embedded in the introduction's implicit statement.

University of Kansas Center for Research on Learning May, 1997

continues

Strategies for Enhancing Text Problem Areas (con't)

Possible Problem Area	Teacher Strategies
Main Parts and Terms ❑ Students cannot differentiate main headings from subheadings and sub/subheadings.	✔Direct students to examine the size, shape, color, & placement of headings to help identify types of headings. ✔Teach students the outline notations, symbols, and patterns. ✔Guide students through the outlining process.
❑ Students cannot diagram the headings into content map form.	✔Guide students through the mapping process. ✔Provide a content map.
❑ Students have difficulty changing headings into questions.	✔Guide students through the process of formulating questions. ✔Provide students with a list of questions and have them match them to appropriate headings.
❑ Students cannot find key terms in the chapter. ❑ Students cannot find definitions of key terms.	✔Direct students to look for: words highlighted in bold print words footnoted at bottom of each page words noted in margins a list at the end of the chapter a glossary. ✔Identify key terms and list on chalkboard.
❑ Students' limited background knowledge/experience makes understanding of key terms/concepts difficult.	✔Pre-teach vocabulary critical to understanding key concepts in the chapter. ✔Have students create vocabulary cards with terms on one side and definitions on the reverse side. For ESL students both languages may be used to facilitate understanding. Use cards to create concept/content maps, as a self-testing tool, etc.
❑ Students cannot relate enrichment features to appropriate headings.	✔Guide students through process.

University of Kansas Center for Research on Learning May, 1997

Strategies for Enhancing Text Problem Areas (con't)

Possible Problem Area	Teacher Strategies
Summary ❑ The chapter does not contain a summary	✔Check introduction and review questions for summary information. ✔Using the information gained through the survey process *(intro, headings, .review questions, etc.)* have students write their own summaries. ✔Summarize the chapter for students.
❑ Students have difficulty paraphrasing the summary because it is too long or summary statements are embedded in the text.	✔Segment the summary to focus students on smaller units of information. ✔Identify words in the text that cue a summary. ✔Summarize the chapter for students.
❑ No review/study questions are provided.	✔Provide students with review/study questions. ✔Guide students through process of formulating review questions based on what they have learned from their survey of the rifle, headings, introductions, etc.
❑ The review/study questions do not review the most important ideas in the chapter.	✔Identify types of information targeted by questions. ✔Provide questions reviewing most important information in the chapter. ✔Guide students in formulating appropriate questions.

University of Kansas Center for Research on Learning May, 1997